*Creolization
in the
Americas*

NUMBER
THIRTY-TWO:
*The Walter
Prescott Webb*
Memorial
Lectures

By David Buisseret
Daniel H. Usner, Jr.
Mary L. Galvin
Richard Cullen Rath
J. L. Dillard

Creolization in the Americas

Introduction by David Buisseret

Edited by David Buisseret and Steven G. Reinhardt

Published for

the University of Texas

at Arlington by

Texas A&M

University Press

COLLEGE STATION

Copyright © 2000
by the University of Texas
at Arlington
Manufactured
in the
United States of America
All rights reserved
First edition

The paper used in this book
meets the minimum requirements
of the American National Standard
for Permanence of Paper
for Printed Library Materials,
Z39.48-1984.
Binding materials
have been chosen for durability.

Library of Congress Cataloging-in-Publication Data

Creolization in the Americas / by David Buisseret . . . [et al.] ; introduction by
David Buisseret ; edited by David Buisseret and Steven G. Reinhardt.—1st ed.
  p. cm. — (The Walter Prescott Webb memorial lectures ; 32)
  Includes bibliographical references.
  ISBN 0-89096-949-3 (cloth) — ISBN 1-58544-101-5 (pbk.)
  1. America—Ethnic relations. 2. Creoles—America—History. 3. Intercultural
communication—America—History. 4. Culture diffusion—America—History.
  5. Acculturation—America—History. I. Buisseret, David. II. Reinhardt,
Steven G., 1949– III. Series.

E29.A1 C74 2000
303.48′2′097—dc21
00-029934

TO
Kenneth R.
Philp
HISTORY
DEPARTMENT
CHAIR
(1987–99)

Contents

Preface ix

Introduction 3
DAVID BUISSERET

*The Process of Creolization
in Seventeenth-Century Jamaica* 19
DAVID BUISSERET

"The Facility Offered by the Country":
The Creolization of Agriculture
in the Lower Mississippi Valley 35
DANIEL H. USNER, JR.

Decoctions for Carolinians:
The Creation of a Creole Medicine Chest
in Colonial South Carolina 63
MARY L. GALVIN

Drums and Power:
Ways of Creolizing Music in Coastal South Carolina
and Georgia, 1730–90 99
RICHARD CULLEN RATH

*The Evidence for Pidgin/Creolization
in Early American English* 131
J. L. DILLARD

Preface

When we were casting about for a theme around which the thirty-second annual Walter Prescott Webb Memorial Lectures could be organized, we realized—quite suddenly—that we had both, in fact, been much concerned with the phenomenon of "creolization" in our previous lives, even if we had not always called it that. Steven Reinhardt, as curator of French manuscripts at the Louisiana Historical Center of the Louisiana State Museum, had edited *The Sun King: Louis XIV and the New World* (1984) and had acted as assistant editor for *Napoleon and America* (1988); both of these exhibition catalogs had been concerned to some degree with the creolization of French cultural practices in Louisiana.

David Buisseret, who also, as it happens, began life as a historian of the French ancien régime, had experienced creolization firsthand during his time in the Department of History at the University of the West Indies (1964–80) and had then, at the Newberry Library, directed four National Endowment for the Humanities–sponsored summer institutes in what were called "Transatlantic encounters" between 1985 and 1988. These institutes revealed, among other things, the great enthusiasm among younger scholars for creolizing studies, particularly as they concern the Iberian world.

So it was with much enthusiasm that we invited four scholars to Arlington for the Webb lectures in March, 1997. They were asked to tackle various problems in the history of "creolization": its origins, the problem of the contemporary and modern meanings of the term, and the various manifestations of the complex, continuing process of cultural exchange and adaptation that began when Africans, Amerindians, and Europeans came into contact with each other. While the authors may vary in their approaches and, in some respects, their conclusions, they essentially agree that the notion of cultural syncretism—whether described as acculturation or creolization—is a conceptual tool of crucial importance for analyzing the interchange that occurred between peoples of the continents bordering the Atlantic Ocean.

Contributors to the volume are drawn from across the transatlantic world, from England (via Jamaica) to Louisiana and Texas. Daniel H. Usner, Jr., a native of New Orleans, is professor of history at Cornell University. He is the author of *Indians, Settlers, and Slaves in a Frontier Exchange Economy: The Lower Mississippi Valley before 1783* (1992), which won the Institute of Early American History and Culture's Jamestown Prize as well as the American Historical Association's John H. Dunning Prize. More recently he has published *American Indians in the Lower Mississippi Valley: Social and Economic Histories* (1998).

Mary L. Galvin, cowinner of the 1997 Webb-Smith Essay Competition, is lecturer in the departments of history and black studies at the University of California, Los Angeles, where she works under the direction of Gary B. Nash. She is currently completing her analysis of cultural evolution entitled "Piecing Together a Colonial Quilt: Creolization in Early South Carolina."

Richard Cullen Rath, cowinner of the 1997 Webb-Smith Essay Competition, holds a Ph.D. in history from Brandeis University where his dissertation examined the ways that early Americans expressed their attitudes toward sound. In 1993 he published "African Music in Seventeenth-Century Jamaica: Cultural Transit and Transition" in *The William and Mary Quarterly*. He later published "Echo and Narcissus: The Afrocentric Pragmatism of W. E. B. Du Bois" in the *Journal of American History* (1997), an article based on an earlier essay that had won the Louis Pelzer Award. In spring, 2000, he lectured on "Soundscapes of Early America" at the Omahundro Institute of Early American History and Culture at Williamsburg, Virginia. Rath currently is visiting lecturer at Hamilton College in New York.

J. L. Dillard, a native of Grand Saline, Texas, is a widely acknowledged expert on black English. He is the author of numerous books published in the United States and Europe, including *Black English, Its History and Usage in the United States* (1972); *Perspectives on Black English* (1974); *Towards a Social History of American English* (1985); and *A History of American English* (1992).

On behalf of the University of Texas at Arlington's (UTA) history department, the editors would like to acknowledge several benefactors and friends of the Walter Prescott Webb Memorial Lecture Series, which was inaugurated in 1965 by Will Holmes, Harold Hollingsworth, and E. C. Barksdale. In the 1970s and 1980s, under the leadership of Richard G. Miller and Stanley H. Palmer (successors to Barksdale as department chair), the lecture series and publications grew in stature and gained a national reputation. The lectures are published by means of a generous endowment from C. B. Smith, Sr., of Austin, a graduate of UTA and a former student of Walter Prescott Webb at the University of Texas at Austin. Smith also provided funds for the annual prize given for the best essay(s) on the year's theme. Additional support is provided by a generous grant from the Rudolf Hermann's Endowment for the Liberal Arts. Thanks also go to Jenkins and Virginia Garrett of Fort Worth, who have long shown both loyalty and generosity to UTA's special collections library and history department. Stephanie Cole and Alusine Jalloh, our colleagues in the department, deserve thanks for assisting in judging the essays submitted for the Webb-Smith Essay Competition. Finally, we would like to acknowledge the support provided by UTA's president, Robert E. Witt, and the invaluable guidance and dedication of the history department's former chair, Kenneth R. Philp.

*Creolization
in the
Americas*

Introduction

David Buisseret

Historians and anthropologists have long been trying to establish a theoretical framework for the syncretic process by which, as all would acknowledge, a truly New World came into being in those regions that the sixteenth-century Europeans prematurely called their "New World." In 1938 Melville Herskovits provided a general overview of the problem in his *Acculturation: The Study of Culture*. He was concerned in part to counter the arguments of the sociologist Franklin Frazier, who, as Richard Rath notes in chapter 4 of this volume, had denied the possibility of any African influences surviving the Middle Passage. However, Herskovits also set out a full analysis of the concept of acculturation, offering reviews of many of the current theories.[1]

Most of these theories, as he noted, more properly described "assimilation" than "acculturation," for they assumed that the process implied the adjustment of one culture to a "superior" one. Herskovits allowed for the possibility of acculturation being mutual, but it was not a point upon which he insisted. Subsequent commentators, down to the present day, have generally assumed that "acculturation" involves a one-way transfer; Mechal Sobel, for instance, wrote in 1987 of "acculturated Africans" without allowing for the possibility of "acculturated Europeans." In the same way Robert Hoover in 1989 wrote that "among the historically known instances of directed culture change, the enculturation of Native Americans into the European lifeway is probably the most significant in terms of its implications for global development." It is true that he also wrote, later in the same article, that "acculturation was not entirely unidirectional," but the thrust of his argument was that we need to study Native American adaptations to "the European lifeway."[2]

Often this argument is couched in terms of a "dominant donor culture" imposing itself upon an inferior (supine?) lifestyle. This concept is exemplified by George Foster's *Culture and Conquest*, in which a truly remarkable range of sources is pressed into service to answer three questions:

1. How can we conceptualize and describe the profile of a dominant donor culture that impinges on a less complex society?
2. What are the selective processes that create this profile?
3. How does a dominant culture, as it is manifest in a contact situation, work to develop new hybrid cultures?[3]

Foster develops his argument around these questions, dealing with a huge range of activities from language to city planning. At one stage this mound of evidence compels him to admit that "in areas of high culture, and especially in Mexico, it is well to bear in mind that, although we tend to think only in terms of Indians acculturating to Spanish ways, there were in fact two recipient groups in process of change: Indian and Spanish."[4] However, with this admission made, Foster goes back to his account of how the "donor culture" functioned; it is as if he, like most of his contemporaries, simply could not escape from the dominant (donor)–dominated (recipient) model, in spite of what the evidence might frequently suggest.

Writing in 1976, Sidney Mintz and Richard Price made a determined attempt to leave the shortcomings of "acculturation" models behind. With the object of offering "a general anthropological approach to the study of Afro-American cultural history," they began by asserting that "no group, no matter how well equipped or how free to choose, can transfer its way of life and the accompanying beliefs and values intact, from one locale to another." This was to admit, in New World cases, that the Europeans, the "donor culture," did not perhaps have a cultural continuity as unblemished as some had postulated (though at the same time Mintz and Price did not believe with Herskovits that African customs survived the Middle Passage largely intact). Coming to the specific case of New World colonies, the authors set out their argument like this: "the so-called creole culture of the plantation colonies began to be forged during the earliest interaction of Europeans and Africans, . . . and the processes of cultural formation were neither unilateral—the imposition of European forms upon passive African recipients—nor homogeneous." They thus declared their difference from what they conceived to be the common wisdom, that "transferred cultural materials weighed much more heavily in favor of the Europeans than of the Africans."⁵

The views of Mintz and Price were in some ways adopted by James Axtell, in whose book *The European and the Indian* we read that "no study of acculturation in colonial America would be complete without giving equal consideration to the question of how English culture was altered by its contacts with native America." Axtell was concerned with Anglo-Indian contact, rather than with the Anglo-African contacts primarily studied by Mintz and Price, but he essentially agreed with them in rejecting the idea of donor and recipient cultures, insisting, for instance, that "from the time the first colonists rowed ashore, they began to borrow items of native material culture."⁶

In the works of Axtell and of Mintz and Price we have therefore escaped from the one-sided definition associated with the words "acculturation" or (worse) "assimilation." However, there seem to be weaknesses in their theories, particularly in regard to their applicability to all New World societies. For example, Axtell was primarily concerned with Indian societies, and Mintz and Price with African American ones, whereas a general theory needs to take both (and indeed eventually new arrivals from such regions as China and India) into account. A general theory also needs to emphasize the influence of environment, considered from the point of view not only of climate and topography but also of available materials for buildings and objects of material culture.

The Concept of "Creolization"

We therefore propose that the concept of "creolization" might usefully replace the older notions of "acculturation" and "assimilation." "Creolization" as a noun has long been used among students of language, and the adjectival and verbal forms of the word, together with the noun "creole," have a long history, enabling us to define its central meaning with some precision.⁷ As a noun, "creole" referred to people born in America of European or of African origins. Thus we might speak of the languishing creoles of Louisiana, or indeed of those African creole slaves who were thought by planters to be less dangerous than slaves freshly arrived from Africa. The adjectival form is commonly applied in everyday parlance; we know, for instance, what is meant by cre-

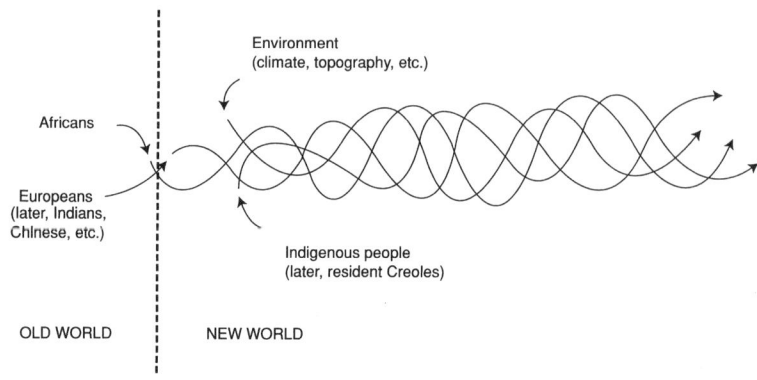

Fig. 1. The Process of Creolization

ole cuisine and creole dialects. The verb form, "to creolize," is much rarer but is defined by the *Oxford English Dictionary* as "to spend the day in a delectable state of apathy," for the English long had the idea that life in the tropics involved an agreeable languor.

All these forms of the word have in common the idea of describing something that is born or developed in the New World, and this is at the heart of the concept of creolization. It describes that "syncretic expression" in which new cultural forms came to life in the New World, just as in the Old World, for instance, English forms emerged from the fusion of Anglo-Saxon and Norman, or Christian forms emerged from a fusion of pagan and apostolic beliefs.[8] The process is probably best described in diagrammatic form (see fig. 1).

On the left are the incoming groups, each with its cultural baggage. At the top are the environmental factors briefly described above, and at the bottom are the influences of the indigenous peoples and later of the resident creoles. It is the interaction of these forces that produces the phenomenon known as creolization and the emergence of creole societies.

Many questions suggest themselves as we reflect upon this model. To start with, do we assume contact influences between Africans and Europeans before and during the Middle Passage? Of course, we have to take such influences into account, some writers even insisting that there already existed in West Africa a sort of creolizing society born of the interaction between native

African rulers, slaves often brought from the interior, and the European factors.[9] Another problem that suggests itself is the role of the indigenous peoples; they are a crucial part of the process, but can they be said eventually to be creolized? To the extent that they will now be part of a newly creolized society, the answer is affirmative. Indeed, sometimes there was even a special name for such creolized natives; in one region of Mexico they were known as "Ladinos."[10] Finally, we have to note the eventual influence of resident creoles, who must have played a powerful role in the acculturative process.

Creolization, as defined in this diagram, was not a voluntary activity. We entirely agree with Mintz and Price and with Axtell that the adaptive pressures were omnipresent and irresistible, even if a person or group tried to resist them. In the Spanish world it was thus impossible for a *criollo*, however well placed, to take on all the characteristics of the *peninsulares*, which indeed, like all cultural phenomena, were in a state of flux. A seventeenth-century gentleman of Virginia might wish and think himself still to be an English gentleman, but in fact he would speak slightly differently, eat differently, dress differently, and in short be different from those cousins who had stayed in England (and who, incidentally, would themselves have changed from the days when our Virginian's forebears had emigrated). It goes without saying that Franco-Canadians rapidly became different from those who continued to speak the French of Touraine.

Factors Influencing the Rate of Creolization

Many authors have tried to assess the elements leading to a faster or slower rate of creolization within any given group. One of these elements is, as Mary Galvin puts it in chapter 3 of this volume, "the newcomer's sense of self-importance relative to the indigenous population." The English in Jamaica after 1655, for instance, had a considerable contempt for their Spanish predecessors and so consciously resisted imitating them in the creolizing process. Many of the French in Canada, on the other hand, do not seem to have felt any innate superiority over their Indian neighbors, and so they relatively rapidly fell in with many of their cultural traits. Similarly, the Franciscan friars who first arrived in Mexico often felt a sort of kinship with the natives, taking care to learn their languages and to adopt some of their customs.[11]

Of course, a sense of self-importance often went along with material abundance, and it is clear that colonists well stocked from the metropolis would be less likely to adopt local habits and diets than would colonists who were destitute. During their starving first years the English in New England were quick to adopt local foods.[12] Once they began to run short of beef in Jamaica, they were quick to learn the virtues of turtle meat. In rather the same way, rich colonists tended to build houses without much regard for local conditions, whereas poor colonists were quickly obliged to adopt local materials and building techniques.[13] Of course, some buildings were so well defined in their functions—such as fortifications and most factories—that the infiltration of local techniques and materials was unlikely.

The situation in which immigrants arrived also played a role. Whereas many Africans arrived in a state of bewildered destitution, some European groups arrived as relatively coherent bodies and, as in parts of English North America, long succeeded in resisting local influences.[14] It mattered, too, how closely the new land resembled the colonists' original homes. Many Spaniards were able to adjust to conditions in Central America with a minimum of initial adaptation, since its climate and soils were rather like those of parts of Spain. On the other hand, the French in Canada had to adopt many Indian customs in order to survive their first few harsh winters. Numbers were also important. In parts of Spanish America the numbers of Spaniards were soon comparable to those of the indigenous inhabitants. However, in much of the Caribbean the Europeans came to be heavily outnumbered by the African slaves, whose influence thus came to bear heavily on such areas as food and speech since throughout the Americas there was almost constant interaction between the various groups.

Some Examples of Creolization

So that the concept of creolization can be made clearer, some examples of the process taken from different regions and different areas of culture will be examined. Architecture, for instance, is an area in which creolizing influences have been studied. In particular, George Kubler has demonstrated how the Franciscan churches of New Mexico and California show different degrees of creolization depending upon the strength and persistence of indigenous architectural traditions. These were strong in New

Mexico, with the consequence that the Spanish style received considerable native variations. However, they were weak in California, where the Spanish style was consequently purer (i.e., there was a lesser degree of creolization). In the postconquest Andes, Daniel Gade found a high degree of creolization among the folk dwellings—what he calls a "melding of traditions"; this is entirely understandable in terms of a society of want. For James Lockhart, the monastery complexes built in Mexico during the first century after Spanish arrival showed a "mixed Hispanic-indigenous tradition," which tended to fade into a more purely European style after the middle of the seventeenth century.[15]

In a careful study of colonial-period Mayan life at Tipu (Belize), Elizabeth Graham found that "the colonial pattern of building represents far more of a break with Maya tradition than anticipated," guessing that this was due to close Spanish supervision and perhaps to a breaking of the indigenous generational links. The antecedents of North American "creole architecture" have been studied by Jay Edwards, who concludes that many architectural features of Caribbean houses (and hence of those in the Mississippi Valley) go back to Africa. In describing one of these features, Edwards calls it "a brilliant Italo-African-Iberian syncretism," and the whole development of this building style is a striking example of the process of creolization.[16]

In agriculture, too, there have been useful studies of the process. For example, Axtell has described the way in which the colonists of New England adopted Indian agricultural practices. In chapter 2 of this volume Daniel Usner describes the conflation of Indian and European practices in the Lower Mississippi Valley. The French colonists of North America also adopted Indian crops and cultivation techniques, with the notable exception that in the Illinois country the French settlers seem to have retained a medieval system of crop rotation, as described by Carl Ekberg. In most of Spanish America there was an early melding of European and indigenous crop types and cultivation practices, with some European crops and many European animals ousting their native counterparts. Daniel Gade has studied this process particularly well in the Andes, where, he concludes, as early as 1540 "the bulk of Spanish material culture had landed in Western South America."[17]

Creolization has been particularly apparent in the area of cooking. In analyzing the cuisine of Puerto Rico today, for instance, the television chef Burt Wolf was able to demonstrate convincingly the continuing role of Amerindian, Spanish, and African ingredients and cooking methods. Axtell noted the early adoption of Indian foods by the English settlers of North America, and Kathleen Deagan noted that in Spanish Saint Augustine (Florida) it was in child rearing and food preparation that "acculturation" was most evident, with much less sign of creolization in architectural style or weaponry—the latter being, of course, examples of that type of technical artifact that we earlier noted as being resistant to syncretic development.[18]

Cartography offers peculiarly striking examples of the creolization process in the Americas. Barbara Mundy carefully tracks this process in *The Mapping of New Spain*, as does Michel Antochiw in *Historia Cartográfica de la Península de Yucatán*. Both authors show how the meso-American and Spanish styles came to a fusion, a conclusion reinforced by other recent work.[19]

There have not been many critical studies of dress in the Americas, but it would be surprising if such studies did not point out many examples of creolization. Axtell has mentioned that such was the case for New England. Also there is no doubt that the inhabitants of New France rapidly adopted the deerskin clothes of their Indian neighbors, while the Indians took over many European artifacts. The wealthier Europeans of the West Indies, secure in their revenues from sugar, long resisted modifications to their extremely unsuitable European garb, but their indentured servants soon stripped down to basic garments, and the Africans were soon clad in shirts, trousers, and shifts made from Osnaburg cloth. There were long-lasting indigenous forms of clothing in much of Latin America and some spectacular exchanges with Spain—for instance when the Indians took over much Spanish headgear and the Spaniards adopted the all-purpose poncho.[20]

Language has been the traditional area in which studies of creolization began, and little will be said about it here except to remark that the Americas house an extraordinary number of creole dialects, deriving from combinations of Portuguese, Spanish, French, Dutch, English, and African tongues with various local languages; many of these combinations are recognized as having passed from the stage of pidgin to that of creole languages.[21] In chapter 5 of this volume Professor Dillard carefully considers the evidence for pidgin creolization in early American English.

In literature it would not appear that many stylistic syncretisms appeared in the French- and English-speaking regions. But in the Spanish world, where the indigenous peoples were introduced early to Castilian language and literature, there have been many creolizing works, such as the famous letter of Guaman Poma, which has been extensively studied by Rolena Adorno. Sometimes, as in the highland region of Guatemala studied by Robert Hill, the adoption of European writing by indigenous peoples was part of a strategy for maintaining a degree of cultural autonomy.[22]

Medicine is another area in which creolization has been exceptionally frequent and varied. In this collection of essays chapters 1 and 3 have something to say about such syncretism in Jamaica and South Carolina, respectively. Patricia Galloway has recently written about "savage medicine" in Louisiana, concluding that the contribution of indigenous information to French medical knowledge in the eighteenth century has been underestimated.[23] From the beginning of their incursion into the Americas, the Spaniards were centrally interested in what they could learn of a New World pharmacopeia, no doubt deriving much information from the now-lost manuscripts of the early botanist Francisco Hernández.[24] No doubt much anecdotal material could be added to these formal accounts of the relationship between European, Indian, and African medicine, such as the account of the way in which Samuel de Champlain relied upon native informants to provide the medicine with which he treated his men against scurvy during their first testing winter on the Saint Lawrence River in 1608. In truth, given the urgent need to find the best possible cures, medical practices have been one of the most fertile areas of collaboration among people of different cultures.

For a different reason, music has also been remarkably fertile in syncretic developments. In North America the contribution of the Indian peoples does not seem to have been great in this area, but some remarkable collaborations have developed down the centuries between the African and European traditions. Mechal Sobel writes of the European dance styles adopted by some of the slaves of Virginia, who in exchange passed on to their masters the "Congo minuet" and the "Negro jig."[25] In early-nineteenth-century Louisiana, Louis Moreau Gottschalk borrowed melodies played by African musicians in New Orleans's Congo Square to write piano compositions that reflected the creole way of life.[26]

The whole question of creolizing music in coastal South Carolina and Georgia has been closely analyzed by Richard Rath in chapter 4 of this volume.

In South America early collaboration developed in Brazil between the musical traditions of Africa and Europe, and in the Spanish colonies between the indigenous peoples and the Spanish choirmasters. The Spanish friars early appreciated the usefulness of song in the process of conversion and composed *villancicos,* or religious songs, drawing upon the rhythms, dialects, and cultural traditions of Indians and then of African slaves in order to teach Christian beliefs. The names of these masters are not widely familiar, but of late the music of composers such as Bermudez and Gutierrez de Padilla has begun to be sung again by specialist choirs. The tradition of creolized music has lasted down the decades into the time of the eighteenth-century Jesuit *reducciones* in Paraguay and indeed to the present day.[27]

Syncretic combinations were particularly abundant, of course, in religion. Although the French and English divines of North America made little progress in their dialogues with the Indians of those parts, there was a remarkable series of exchanges in the early sixteenth century between the friars of New Spain and their Nahua interlocutors, brilliantly described by Louise Burkhart. She concludes that the result of the friars' work was "a partially Christianized ethnography, corresponding to the partially Nahuatized Christianity that constituted the other side of the dialogue," and that the resultant catechistic literature was not simply a body of Christian writings but "the residue of a dynamic interaction between European and Nahuatl culture." Her work, in fact, provides a textbook example of a vigorous creolizing process at work. A quite different but no less vigorous process took place in the Caribbean, where various forms of African animist belief combined with Christianity to form such religions as Shango in Trinidad or the more purely African *cumina* in Jamaica.[28]

There is, then, a vast range of examples of the creolizing process, even without taking into account such areas of human activity as art, law, material culture, military organization, politics, or social structures, for which there is not space here. Granted, though, that this process has been almost universal in the Americas since the arrival of the Europeans and Africans, we must now ask if it is possible to define more closely the stages of its development.

Stages of Creolization

For the Swiss scholar Urs Bitterli, cultural "encounters between European and non-European cultures" may be divided into four phases: initial contacts, collisions, relationships, and (after 1800) "cultural intermingling." The first two categories are easy to understand; clearly, the Portuguese of West Africa in the fifteenth century were at the phase of initial contact, and Columbus on Santo Domingo initiated the phase of conflict in the New World. The stage of "relationship" is characterized by the French *coureurs de bois* in seventeenth-century Canada or by the early Portuguese in Brazil. But it is not easy to see why Bitterli would deny to this stage the description of his fourth phase, "cultural intermingling." Surely the coureurs de bois were prime examples of such exchange, or creolization as we have called it, and there are many more such examples before Bitterli's starting date of 1800.[29]

Francis Jennings offers a model including six phases of encounter: contact, catastrophic depopulation, reordering of dominance-dependence groups, gradual revival of population, acculturation processes, and "establishment of a large society in which all participant groups have undergone cultural change, and in which subcultures continue to display vestigial features of the originating ethnic groups."[30] Jennings's model, which owes much to his preoccupation with North American Indians, has the great merit of shifting our attention away from initial contacts and emphasizing that the process of creolization continues over the long term to affect all groups. Perhaps an example of this development would be the way in which African music forms, after gestating for many years in the Lower Mississippi regions, eventually came to have a powerful and continuing influence upon the common music of the United States.

In *The Nahuas after the Conquest* James Lockhart draws upon a vast range of knowledge to offer a table setting out the three stages of development in various categories such as language, labor mechanisms, and government. These three stages last from 1519 to about 1550, from then to about 1650, and from then to 1800, respectively. On the whole, Lockhart seems to agree with

Foster's argument that over time the Spanish forms tended to predominate.[31]

The most recent attempt to suggest a periodization of the creolization process is the work of Susan Ball.[32] This young scholar has suggested a tripartite division for what she calls "The phase one colonization model," dealing with "the very beginnings of the colonization effort." Here she identifies three processes, called "reduction, configuration, and exchange." Reduction involves the shedding and simplification of cultural traits in view of impending multicultural contact. This process is hard to describe, but it is easy to concede that Africans and Europeans coming to the New World may, indeed, have divested themselves of much cultural baggage on the way. The phase of configuration takes in the phase by which elements within a group "are reorganized to meet the needs of people in the colonial or contact situation." The final phase, exchange, comprehends what we have called initial creolization.

From the point of view of our model, Ball offers helpful suggestions about how the initial stages of the process might be more precisely described (notably by including the idea of "reduction"), and Jennings reminds us that the process needs to be tracked far beyond the initial century of contact, into a period when the balance of power between the various cultures may go through many unexpected changes. In terms of general New World history, Jennings may offer a corrective to the ideas of Foster and Lockhart, who were particularly impressed by the weight of the Spanish cultural contribution. Over the centuries perhaps the demographic weight of the Indian cultures begins to tell more and more, just as the demographic weight of the African cultures is more and more apparent in the Caribbean.

Conclusion

In reflecting as broadly as possible on the process of creolization, we are struck by the way in which the Spanish, Portuguese (the latter are rather neglected in this work), and French immigrants seemed more open to intercultural contact than did the English. In the case of the French, it was no doubt a combination of their small numbers and the harshness of the climate that made them so accommodating in Canada. But the Spaniards and Portuguese seem to have had an openness to other cultures that is perhaps explained by their origins. After all, both their societies were recent syncretisms in the fifteenth century, when they were in the process of absorbing the Moorish and Jewish cultures—even though they would later try to repudiate both. Perhaps the experience of syncretism in the Old World imperceptibly prepared them for their experiences in the new one.

Our model of creolization seems to be more inclusive than are some past models, for ours includes both the indigenous and the African contributions and insists upon the role of the environment in modifying the culture patterns of all concerned. Our model may still not be inclusive enough in its categories, for it has nothing to say about the creolization of flora and fauna—about the massive exchange of species that gave rise to entirely new "creole" landscapes. This model may also be insufficiently inclusive in time, for some scholars insist that we should think of an "entire creolizing spectrum" along which "a conversation between cultures goes on." As the same scholar adds, what would life in Sweden be like without reggae and the Japanese model? For Ulf Hannertz, "we are all being creolized."[33] That is no doubt true, but it seems wiser to confine the notion of creolization to the first two or three centuries of syncretic interaction in the Americas, leaving other times and places to develop their own definitions and terminology for what is indeed part of a universal process.

Notes

1. Melville Herskovits, *Acculturation: The Study of Culture* (New York: J. J. Augustin, 1938); see Franklin Frazier, *The Negro Family in the United States* (1939; rev. ed., Chicago: University of Chicago Press, 1948), as well as Melville Herskovits, *The Myth of the Negro Past* (Boston: Beacon Press, 1958).
2. Mechal Sobel, *The World They Made Together: Black and White Values in Eighteenth-Century Virginia* (Princeton, N.J.: Princeton University Press, 1987); Robert Hoover, "Spanish-Native Interaction and Acculturation in the Alta California Missions," in *Columbian Consequences*, ed. David Hurst Thomas, vol. 1 (Washington, D.C.: Smithsonian Institution Press, 1989–91), pp. 395–406.
3. George Foster, *Culture and Conquest: America's Spanish Heritage* (Chicago: Quadrangle Books, 1960).
4. Ibid., p. 227.
5. Sidney Mintz and Richard Price, *An Anthropological Approach to the Afro-American Past: A Caribbean Perspective* (Philadelphia: Institute for the Study of Human Issues, 1976; republished, 1992), p. 1.
6. James Axtell, *The European and the Indian* (New York and Oxford: Oxford University Press, 1981), p. 272.

7. Often in attempts to establish the stages of pidginization and creolization; see, for instance, Dell Hymes, ed., *Pidginization and Creolization of Languages* (Cambridge: Cambridge University Press, 1971).

8. The phrase quoted is that of Serge Gruzinski in *The Conquest of Mexico* (Cambridge, UK: Polity Press, 1993).

9. See Urs Bitterli, *Cultures in Conflict: Encounters between European and Non-European Cultures, 1492–1800* (Stanford, Calif.: Stanford University Press, 1989), pp. 52–69.

10. Janine Gasco, "Indian Survival and Ladinoization on Colonial Soconosco," in *Columbian Consequences*, vol. 3, pp. 301–18.

11. Sidney Mintz has addressed the general problem in "The Socio-historical Background to Pidginization and Creolization," in *Pidginization and Creolization of Languages*, pp. 481–96. Louise Burkhart writes about the early Franciscans in *The Slippery Earth: Nahua-Christian Moral Dialogue in Sixteenth-Century Mexico* (Tucson: University of Arizona Press, 1989), pp. 15–18.

12. Axtell, *The European and the Indian*, pp. 292–93.

13. See the numerous examples in David Buisseret, *Historic Architecture of the Caribbean* (London and Kingston, Jamaica: Heinemann, 1980).

14. Some persistent survivals are set out in David Hackett Fisher, *Albion's Seed: Four British Folkways in America* (New York: Oxford University Press, 1989).

15. George Kubler, "Two Models of Franciscan Architecture: New Mexico and California," *Gazette des Beaux-Arts* 23 (1943): 39–48; Daniel Gade, "Landscape, System and Identity in the Post-Conquest Andes," *Annals of the Association of American Geographers* 82 (1992): 460–77; James Lockhart, *The Nahuas after the Conquest* (Stanford, Calif.: Stanford University Press, 1992), tab. 10.4.

16. Elizabeth Graham, "Archaeological Insights into Colonial-Period Maya Life at Tipu, Belize," in *Columbian Consequences*, vol. 3, pp. 319–35; Jay Edwards, "The Origins of Creole Architecture," *Winterthur Portfolio* 29 (1994): 155–89.

17. Axtell, *The European and the Indian*, pp. 294–95; Carl J. Ekberg, *French Roots in the Illinois Country: The Mississippi Frontier in Colonial Times* (Urbana: University of Illinois Press, 1998); Gade, "Landscape, System and Identity," p. 462.

18. "San Juan," in the series *A Taste for Travel* (video, New York, 1996); Axtell, *The European and the Indian*, pp. 292–93; Kathleen Deagan, "Mestizaje in Colonial St. Augustine," *Ethnohistory* 20 (1973): 55–77.

19. See Barbara Mundy, *The Mapping of New Spain: Indigenous Cartography and the Maps of the Relaciones Geográficas* (Chicago: University of Chicago Press, 1996); Michel Antochiw, *Historia Cartográfica de la Península de Yucatán* (Campeche, Mex.: Centro de Investigación y de Estudios Avanzados del I.P.N., 1994); David Buisseret, "Meso-American and Spanish Cartography: An Unusual Example of Syncretic Development," in *The Mapping of the Entradas into the Greater Southwest*, ed. Dennis Reinhartz and Gerald Saxon (Norman: University of Oklahoma Press, 1998), pp. 30–55.

20. Axtell, *The European and the Indian*, p. 297; see, for instance, George Foster, *Culture and Conquest*, pp. 87–103.

21. On this topic see Mervyn Alleyne, "Acculturation and the Cultural Matrix of Creolization," in *Pidginization and Creolization of Languages*, pp. 169–86.

22. Rolena Adorno, *Guaman Poma: Writing and Resistance in Colonial Peru* (Austin: University of Texas Press, 1986); Robert Hill, "The Social Uses of Writing

among the Colonial Cakchique Maya: Nativism, Resistance and Innovation," in *Columbian Consequences,* vol. 3, pp. 283–99.

23. Patricia Galloway, "Savage Medicine: Du Pratz and the Eighteenth-Century French Medical Practice," in *France in the New World,* ed. David Buisseret (East Lansing: Michigan State University Press, 1998), pp. 107–18.

24. See David Goodman, *Power and Penury: Government, Technology and Science in Philip II's Spain* (Cambridge and New York: Cambridge University Press, 1988), pp. 234–38.

25. Sobel, *The World They Made Together,* p. 167.

26. See Frederick S. Starr, *Bamboula: The Life and Times of Louis Moreau Gottschalk* (New York: Oxford University Press, 1995).

27. See, for instance, *Native Angels,* a compact disc published in 1997 by the San Antonio Vocal Arts Ensemble; see the concert of "Baroque Music from the Missions in Paraguay and Bolivia" sung at Techne, Ill., in May, 1995, by The Cathedral Singers.

28. In Burkhart, *Slippery Earth,* pp. 184–93; see Alleyne, "Acculturation and the Cultural Matrix," p. 181.

29. See Bitterli, *Cultures in Conflict,* pp. 20–51.

30. Francis Jennings in *The Invasion of America: Indians, Colonialism, and the Cant of Conquest* (Chapel Hill: University of North Carolina Press, 1975), p. 207.

31. Lockhart, *Nahuas after the Conquest,* tab. 10.1, p. 428.

32. See Susan Ball, "The Phase One Colonization Model," *Forum on European Expansion and Global Interaction Newsletter* 3, no. 1 (spring, 1992): 2–6.

33. Ulf Hannertz, "The World in Creolization," *Africa* 57 (1987): 546.

The Process of Creolization in Seventeenth-Century Jamaica

David Buisseret

For many years historians of many kinds were unwilling to address the question of creolization in Jamaica. Writing out of the colonial tradition, Frank Cundall could observe, with unusual obtuseness, that "Jamaica's landscape, religion, laws and politics are English," thus obviating the possibility of other contributions. From a radically different standpoint, Orlando Patterson came to much the same conclusion; for him, the African people who came over as slaves were simply too brutalized to have carried much cultural baggage with them. The whole problem of creolization was set in a new light by the publication in 1971 of Edward Brathwaite's brilliant work *The Development of Creole Society in Jamaica 1770–1820*.[1]

Brathwaite demonstrated not only that there was a viable and many-sided culture among the slaves, but also that the slaves' culture had in many areas of human activity fused with the culture of the masters, producing something quite new. The emergence of this "creole society" was the work not only of mostly anonymous uprooted Africans, but also of deracinated Englishmen such as Samuel Long; together they developed new forms of language, architecture, food and drink, and medicine, for example. These forms often owed much to Africa and much to England, but they were no longer either purely African or purely English.

Parallels to the developments described by Brathwaite exist in the history of other New World societies: for example, the French and the Indians in Canada; the English and the Africans on the east coast of the United States; the Spaniards and the Aztecs in Central America; and the Portuguese and the Africans in Brazil. Indeed, it now seems that creolization is a universal New World phenomenon, inevitably affecting all immigrants from the moment they step ashore. It would now seem that Brathwaite had understated his case and that marked evidence of creolization could be found well before the eighteenth century—indeed, from the very start of British presence in 1655, when they seized the island from the Spaniards.[2]

The British army of invasion consisted of roughly seven thousand men who had come directly from England, together with another thousand levied from the eastern Caribbean islands of Saint Kitts, Nevis, and Montserrat. In the eastern Caribbean the latter troops would have been thoroughly conversant with local cultural patterns, some of them inherited from the Arawaks. In 1627 a group of thirty-two Arawaks had willingly sailed from Essequibo to Barbados and had taught the new colonists how to cultivate tropical plants. The colonists had repaid them for this signal service by enslaving them.[3]

The British army, eight thousand strong, overwhelmed Jamaica's inhabitants, who could muster only a few hundred ill-armed militiamen and therefore could not contemplate open resistance. Most made their way to Cuba, while bands of African-Spanish guerrillas took to the hills. Here they carried on a running war against the invaders, who soon lost about half their number to disease. By 1660 there were about four thousand British people left, and in that year one of the leading guerrilla captains, Juan de Bolas, came over to them, thus effectively ending formal African-Spanish resistance.[4] Presumably the British could have learned a good deal about Spanish cultural patterns from Juan de Bolas and his followers; Sir Hans Sloane mentions that he particularly sought out these "Blacks and Indians" because of their knowledge of local flora.[5] The British also perhaps made contact with some Portuguese Jews who were resident on the north side and may never have fled.[6] At all events, from the start the soldiers who became the first English settlers had the opportunity to know something about the distinctive cultural ways of the Caribbean.

Food

At first the army tried to survive on European staples held in the storeships that accompanied them. However, these supplies of English (and often Irish) cheese, butter, bread, beer, fruit, and vegetables proved to have their disadvantages. Because cheese and butter did not travel well, some had to be thrown overboard after only four weeks at sea, and the rest must soon have perished in the relatively hot Jamaican climate. Nor would it be easy to produce butter and cheese on the island, since thirty years after the British occupation, John Taylor observed that only "two or three great plantations" were attempting to do so.⁷

Bread was almost equally difficult to keep from rotting in the humidity encountered both on the voyage and on the island. As the log of H.M.S. *Hunter* notes in a 1676 entry, six weeks outward bound from London, "we surveyed and cast overboard bread rotten and mouldie, 294 pounds."⁸ Similar entries were frequent, and it even proved difficult to make palatable bread on the island from imported wheat flour, which tended to become stale and magotty rapidly. Of course, wheat could not be grown in the tropics, so the English were thus deprived of their chief starch.

Their main drink was beer, and this too traveled badly. Many of the ships' logs mention "stinckinge beere," and neither cider nor ale was any more reliable; as Sloane puts it, "they huff, and fly in this strange climate." In spite of these problems beer, cider, and ale continued to be imported, along with the more reliable (but also more expensive) brandy and Madeira wine.⁹

European fruits and vegetables also presented problems. Onions and peas crossed the Atlantic well but could not be persuaded to grow in Jamaica. Apples and pears were hard to keep during the crossing and even harder to grow before the cooler, wetter foothills of the Blue Mountains had been opened up.

One way and another, much of the food to which the soldiers were accustomed would not be available in Jamaica—neither their preferred drinks, nor their main starch, nor their customary vegetables and fruits. It would seem, though, that they adapted fairly rapidly to local substitutes. For starch they had a wide choice. Cassava had been grown on the island in the time of the Tainos and had been taken over by the Spaniards. The British also used it, making a farina that Sloane describes as workable into oat cakes similar to those of Scotland.¹⁰ This starch was new to the English and also probably new to the Africans, who began arriving on the island in appreciable numbers during the 1660s as the potential of a slave-driven sugar economy became apparent.

Another source of starch was the Taino crop of maize, which had been grown on raised beds, or *conucos*, on the Jamaican plains. The English seem to have regarded maize without much affection, but it was often prepared for slaves and was probably a new crop for them too. It could either be "tosted or boiled," as Sloane puts it.[11] While young corn can be quite good roasted, the slaves rapidly grew tired of it in boiled form and are described by Richard Ligon in Barbados as crying out, "O! O! no more lob-lob."[12] It might be called either lob-lob or loblolly in the West Indies and cornpone or polenta in other parts of the world.

The Africans were well accustomed to eating various forms of yams, which indeed were found on both sides of the Atlantic. This item of the Jamaican diet would, however, have been a novelty for the English. The Africans were also used to eating some form of plantains. These were often roasted and would have been new to the English, as were sweet potatoes. Guinea corn was grown but was usually fed to the poultry. In addition rice was "planted by some Negroes in their own plantations."[13] Presumably rice culture was known in the parts of Africa from which these cultivators came, and the English would have been familiar with it through the Mediterranean trades.

In the near absence of beer and ale, other drinks were pressed into service by the new settlers. Perino, the pulque of modern Mexico, was made from cassava.[14] Mobbie, which was made from sweet potatoes, tasted like new Rhine wine, according to one optimistic commentator.[15] The Spaniards, following the example of the indigenous peoples, had cultivated cocoa, and chocolate became a favorite drink. Coffee was not yet known. Many juices could be made from such fruits as the pineapple, and once sugar cultivation became widespread in the 1660s rum was often available.

The fruit trees of Jamaica were exceptionally abundant and varied. If they could not have their apples and pears, the English could make do with a wide range of citrus, introduced by the Spaniards, and with such indigenous fruits as guava, papaya, and pineapple. They particularly prized pineapple, which was described in an early edition of the *Laws of Jamaica* as "the celebrated pine . . . that incomparable fruit."[16] A range of vegetables also came to supplant the European onions and peas. These included the indigenous lima bean and cho cho (a green marrow-like gourd), together with the African callaloo and akee. On the whole, the Africans probably had to adapt less than the English did to the new range of fruits and vegetables.

Some meat and fish were more or less common to all three regions: England, Africa, and the Caribbean. Beef and goat were used when available, as were the excellent wild hogs. Various kinds of game birds could be shot or trapped, and the streams yielded such delicacies as mullet, eels, and crayfish (the latter often known by the African name *janga*). In addition ocean fish that were more or less familiar on both sides of the Atlantic could be caught; they bred in great numbers in the shallow lagoons around the southern coast.

Even when the meat and fish were more or less familiar, they came to be prepared in new ways, in deference to the tropical heat. Meat was often "jirked," as Sloane puts it; Taylor describes the process like this: "After [the hunters] have slasht it here and there with their knives they put some little salt thereon, after which with smoke they dry it on a barbeque (as we doe red herrings in Europe) and afterward pack it up in cabadge leaves, and this they call jerckt hog, which proveth excellent food, will keep long and yeildeth a good price at Port Royal." Fish underwent a similar process of preservation. As Taylor puts it, "[of this fish] they make a great dish at Port Royal by cutting it into small pieces and frieing it very drie in oyle, and then putting it in a pickle flaurd with spices . . . this fish so ordered they call caveich." Like jerking meat, "escovitching" fish came from the Spaniards and is still commonly used in the Caribbean.[17]

Some of the slaves were used to a diet heavy on meat, and they must often have found the Jamaican food monotonous. Their diet could, however, be supplemented by a variety of proteins, such as the turtle meat upon which the English army largely subsisted at a critical time in 1656. Manatees and alligators were also commonly eaten, as were lizards and some kinds of rats. According to Sloane, the "Indians and negroes" also ate "snakes or serpents." From an early date salted fish seems to have been imported from the New England colonies, for Taylor writes in 1686 of the "old stincking salt fish" that was given to the slaves. This source of protein sometimes became very important, for in some years—for instance, 1686—"plantation provisions begin to fail and European provisions to be very expensive."[18]

What is clear is that both native and imported provisions continued for many years side by side. Probably the rich remained most wedded to the expensive European foods, but it seems clear that all groups had at times to call upon the wide range of creole foods. To complete the dualism, it is also clear that these foods were cooked in European pots and also in African yabbas (an earthenware cooking pot) found on many seventeenth-century archaeological sites. As with the food, so with the drink, for the early inhabitants not only used European and African utensils but completed the trilogy by using the coconut, known to the Tainos and praised by Taylor as forming a "handsome drinking cup."[19]

Dress

There is little visual evidence concerning dress in Jamaica during the seventeenth century, though eventually the lithographers gave us a good idea of what people wore in the last days of slavery.[20] However, the written evidence is fairly abundant and helpful. We know, for instance, that the slaves received a yearly allowance of blue or white Osnaburg, which seems to have been a sort of denim, and that a man often used this to make "a little canvas jacket or britches."[21] The women slaves no doubt used their allowance to make shifts, and both sexes were probably clad rather like the indentured servants, who received similar supplies. The poorer free Europeans seem also to have dressed simply. Taylor describes "a common woman clad only in her smock and linen peticoate, barefooted with shoe or stockins, with a straw hatt and a red tobacco pipe in their mouths, and thus they trampouse about the streets in this their warlike posture, and thus arrayed they will booze a cupp of punch rumly with anyone."[22] It sounds as if they had made some considerable adaptations to the climate, for in England they probably would have worn woolen clothing and some form of footwear.

The wealthier European inhabitants seem to have adapted their clothing much less, to judge by the inventories from Port Royal. Here we find some mention of cotton and linen garments, but there was plenty of wool, and the latest fashions were imported unchanged from London.[23] Dr. Sloane was critical of this disinclination of the wealthier inhabitants to adapt their clothing, writing, "it seems to me that the Europeans do not well, who coming from a cold country, continue to clothe themselves after the same manner as in England, whereas all the inhabitants between the tropics go almost naked, and Negroes and Indians live almost so here."[24]

Architecture

Sloane was equally critical of the way in which the rich English merchants built their houses. At Port Royal, he wrote, "the houses built by the British are for the most part brick, and after the English manner, which are neither cool nor able to withstand the shock of earthquakes."²⁵ For John Taylor, on the other hand, this resolute re-creation of Old England was admirable; he wrote that "the brick buildings here erected by the English are as lofty and butiful as our buildings in London, and glazed with glass windows. The Spanish houses are low timberwork houses thatch'd with palmetto leaves, being but one story high, paved with tiles, having lattice windows and great dores opening with two leaves."²⁶

The contrast between Sloane and Taylor is striking. Taylor, who no doubt represented the common opinion of the island, approved of the destruction of those Spanish houses that had been so well adapted to the climate, and he unthinkingly tended to praise buildings modeled on those of England. Sloane saw much further into the need for adaptation to the climate, even foretelling the massive destruction at Port Royal in the earthquake of 1692. Probably the "lofty and butiful buildings" erected by the English were confined to Port Royal and Spanish Town. On the rest of the island wealthy landowners developed a distinctive type of fortified house, of which a fine example survives at Stokes Hall, though it is now in ruins.²⁷

More modest houses rapidly began developing creole elements: for example, elevated ground floors, louvered galleries, shingled roofs, hurricane shelters, and dormer windows. It is not clear how early such houses were built, but some of these features may have been emerging by the end of the seventeenth century. Local features were abundant even earlier on the humblest houses, built by slaves and indentured servants. Here we might have found buildings rather like those of the Arawaks: forked-stick frame cabins roofed and sided with reed and palm leaf of a type that has survived in parts of the Caribbean down to the present day.

On the whole, wealthy people tended to cling to the European patterns of architecture. Poorer people were obliged to adapt to local conditions—or, in other terms, they experienced rapid creolization. Such adaptations were rare not only in wealthy people's houses but also in buildings that were specific in function. There was, for instance, little evidence of creole adaptation in churches or fortifications. Even the ubiquitous sugar factories were constructed basically following the European mode for in-

Fig. 2. Pierre Menard home near Chester in southern Illinois. A fine example of early French Creole architecture built by slave labor in 1802.

dustrial structures. Once the creole elements became established in domestic architecture, though, they would have a long history, eventually crossing the Gulf of Mexico to influence buildings such as the West Indian raised cottage, which is found as far north as Minnesota (see fig. 2).[28]

We know little about the furniture of seventeenth-century Jamaican houses, but these items would not seem to have differed much from their English counterparts.[29] Indeed, eventually the island became famous for the skill of its cabinetmakers in copying English designs. In one respect, however, there was a major innovation: hammocks came to be widely used. As Sloane puts it, "Hamacas are the common beds of ordinary white people, they were in use among the Indians, and are much cooler than beds, so cool as not to be lain in without clothes, especially if swung, as is usually the custom here." Sloane adds that "Indians and Negroes" normally lay on the floor, as did "ordinary white servants," using some form of mat. It would seem that a type of hammock was also used for babies in Jamaica. As Sloane puts it, "cradles are not us'd very much, but hamacas to be laid in, wherein they are toss'd or swung as if they were in a cradle. They make an engine of wood, as long as the child, a little broader, and a foot and a half high arch'd at the top." Nets were also used, for "the sides and top are covered with gauze to hinder the gnats or mosquitos molesting the child lying under it."[30]

Medicine

Although Sloane made many observations about everyday life, his primary calling was as a physician, and he offers many insights into the nature of doctoring in seventeenth-century Jamaica. It is plain from his main text, and from his case studies, that African medicine was practiced alongside the European methods. He thus describes Sir Henry Morgan's (unavailing) recourse to a "black doctor"; the ideas of "Hercules, a lusty black negro overseer and doctor"; and the skillful way in which a black medicine woman showed him how to remove chiggers.[31]

Sloane showed appreciation for the remedies of the New World, particularly quinine, of which he wrote that "a poor Indian who first taught the cure of an ague, of which the lady of the count of Chinon was sick, overthrew with one simple medicine all the hypotheses and theories of agues." He carefully describes the blood coagulant properties of the "Jamaican Blood Flower" and sets out the antibacterial action of the "contra yerba." He observed the limited range of the slave doctors' herbal remedies, or "simples," noting that in each case they normally took the appropriate substance not as a decoction or distillation, but "in substance," thus perhaps increasing the medicinal effect.[32]

In general Sloane was not an admirer of the medical practices of the "many Indian and Black Doctors," but then modern Western doctors would probably find much fault in Sloane's own ideas. It may be, too, that a whole area of folk medicine, largely practiced by women doctor/nurses and relying extensively upon herbal remedies, remained closed to him. Be that as it may, it is clear that in seventeenth-century Jamaica there was an extensive conflation of European and African practices.[33] The existence of many African cures is also confirmed by the fact that to this day Jamaican and African folk medicine share many ingredients in common.

Taylor has some interesting passages about the effects of Caribbean residence upon Europeans. "Those English children," he writes, "which are born here they call Crebolians (because born on one of the Crebe islands): they grow generally tall and slender, of a spare thin body and pale complexion, having all light flaxen haire, being at the full growth and prime strength att fifteen years old, and seldom live above five and twenty years, for as soone as they are tenteey they begin to decline."[34] It is not clear how much truth there is in Taylor's assessment, for other sources suggest that Jamaican whites who survived infancy might go on to attain a considerable age. There was also the stereotype in England of the West Indian planter as a person with thin arms and legs and a protuberant belly. Perhaps we should think of the seventeenth-century English Jamaicans as somewhat resembling in physical type some of the Appalachian peoples of the present day. The chief characteristic attributed to the creole Africans by the planters was a relative docility in the face of the injustices of the plantation system. Some authors believe, as well, that they tended to grow taller and heavier than their cousins back in Africa, but the evidence on this point is inconclusive.

Language and Music

For different reasons, the evidence about the degree of linguistic creolization during the seventeenth century is also inconclusive, since we have few texts speaking directly to this subject. Such texts only became abundant during the eighteenth century, when plainly African features are discernible in what had by then developed from a pidgin to a creole language. Most commentators would probably agree that by then spoken Jamaican was marked by at least four African-based characteristics. The first of these was the rhythm of the language, variously described as a "broken way of talking" or "a sort of broken English, with an indolent drawing out of the words."[35] Visitors and expatriate planters often remarked on the way in which young white Jamaicans acquired this apparently undesirable way of speaking from the domestic slaves; once acquired, they retained it for life. Second, some frankly African words made their way into the Jamaican lingua franca, eventually perhaps making up about 10 percent of the common vocabulary, or about four hundred words. Words such as "fufu" for cornmeal pone, "janga" for crayfish, and (a different adaptation) "big-eye" for greedy came into common use.[36] Third, some proverbs also seem to have come from Africa; here we think of "cockroach na business wid fowl fight" (the cockroach should not interfere when the chickens are quarreling) or "no cuss gator long mout til unnu cross ribber" (don't criticize the alligator until you are across the river). Finally, African seems prevalent in salty and concise idioms and in exceptionally apt nicknames. Such idioms might include "if life spare" (if the Lord does not take me) and "good cyan done" (you can't get enough of a good thing), still frequently heard.

These Africanisms were added to seventeenth-century English to form a language that was eventually distinctive and quite different from its progenitors in Africa or England (where, of course, the language was in any case also constantly changing through the centuries). The problem is to know how far this process of syncretism had gone by 1700. In the absence of textual evidence, we may suppose that the early pidgin was passed on from creole slaves to new arrivals and that after fifty years or so was becoming well established among both Africans and English people.

We are better able to gauge the nature of the seventeenth-century musical fusion, thanks to the recent work of Richard Rath. His main source is a passage in Sloane's *Voyage* where Dr. Sloane describes how he and a visiting French musician called Baptiste witnessed some music-making by slaves on a Jamaican plantation. According to Rath, this evidence provides "a unique glimpse into the process of creolization among enslaved Africans of known ethnicity." Rath shows how the music (in melody and rhythm), language, and instrumentation of the songs heard by Sloane and Baptiste may be related back to specific areas of Africa, even though they had been subtly changed by the transatlantic crossing. Of the three songs, "Angola" is clearly pidgin, with strong African elements; "Koromanti" is much more fully creolized. As Rath puts it, we have here a specific example of the molding of "the creole cultural language that subsequent unseasoned Africans would have to learn as a second language"—no doubt incorporating into it their own distinctive contributions.[37]

Laws

The Jamaican legal system was, of course, based on that of England, but here, too, distinctive features soon emerged. As Richard Blome puts it, "their laws are assimilated, as near as may be, to those of England."[38] But there was no allowance in English law for formalized slavery, so that a great body of new law came to regulate the behavior of both slaves and indentured servants. One law, cited by Taylor, showed how in the seventeenth century there was provision for a baptized slave to proceed to a different status: "all such Indian or Negroe slaves which are lawfully baptized by a Christian minister, after they are grown to manhood and past age, shall then from the time of their baptism into the Christian church faithfully serve their masters as slaves for the space of seven years and noe longer, which being expired they shall be made free denizens of the island, and enjoy all Christian liberty as aforesaid."[39] It would not seem that this law was ever applied, as the mounting success of the plantation system led to ever more stringent demands upon the slave labor, but it is an interesting example of the way in which English law had to be creolized.

Other examples come from the area that would now be called ecological controls. There was, for instance, to be "no poisoning of rivers with ye bark of ye dogwood tree, tobacco or any other thing" and "no killing of those harmless birds called carrion crows or Jamaican vultures, which are so usefull in devouring carrion carcasses."[40] Thus, although the administration of the judicial system remained resolutely English, with justices of the peace, parish courts, and superior courts in Spanish Town, the actual content of many of the laws had to take account of the distinctive local conditions.

Politics

Much the same was true of the political structure, in which the Jamaican trilogy of governor–council–House of Assembly was held to mirror the English trilogy of king–House of Lords–House of Commons. Of course, the governor ruled not by divine right but at the king's pleasure, and the council consisted not of the ancient lords spiritual and temporal but of the governor's nominees. Still, the comparison was not altogether inappropriate; certainly the members of both the House of Commons and the House of Assembly were elected on a restricted franchise, which excluded the majority of the population.

Trevor Burnard has recently argued that from 1655 to 1780 there was little "native patriotism" in Jamaica, which he sees as dominated by immigrant political interests.[41] This may be true for the eighteenth century, when many substantial planters succeeded in "escaping" to England and when substantial metropolitan military and naval forces strongly influenced Jamaican society and politics. However, it does not seem to be true for much of the seventeenth century, when what has elsewhere been described as "creole patriotism" was much in evidence. The old but excellent work of Agnes Whitson surely demonstrates that although at first the House of Assembly was in the hands of the governor, during the 1670s it began to assert itself.[42] By 1677 half of the members were "old standers" who had come over in 1655, and they were both eager to assert their rights against the Crown (in much the same way as the House of Commons had done) and keen to reduce as far as possible metropolitan influences. Here Whitson provides a most telling quotation: "The mutual dislike of the Creolians, or native-born, and Englishmen increased, and the former, who will not allow themselves to be called 'Englishmen,' carried their jealousy to the length of attempting to exclude Englishmen from the island's offices."[43] What we see here is surely the kind of clash between metropolitan-based governors and local legislatures that took place in many of the northern British colonies and culminated in their independence. By 1728 in Jamaica the House of Assembly had conceded a modest annual revenue, and the reliance on England described by Burnard was getting well established. But in the seventeenth century, and particularly before the disasters of the 1690s—the earthquake at Port Royal in 1692, the French invasion of 1694, and the progressive growth of the Maroons—the House showed a creole patriotism comparable to similar movements in colonies such as Virginia. Perhaps we ought also to take into account the political effects of the establishment of an economic monoculture, which attached Jamaican to England much more closely than most of the North American colonies, with their more varied economic production, could be tied.

Conclusion

It would seem, then, that in many ways Jamaica had developed a well-marked creole culture by 1700. The island had a distinctive cuisine, and its inhabitants dressed differently from their forbears or contemporaries in Africa and England. Their language was a conflation of English and African words, phrases, and rhythms, and their music was taking new shapes, with influences from both Europe and Africa. In both architecture and music the range of practices took into account the tropical environment while containing elements from both the founding peoples. The legal and political structures were recognizably English in origin but were already showing clear signs of independent development. From this evidence it would seem that we are fully justified in speaking of the emergence of many elements of a creole society in seventeenth-century Jamaica.

Notes

1. The quote is by Howard Johnson in chapter 20, volume 6 of the UNESCO *History of the Caribbean* (in press); Orlando Patterson, *The Sociology of Slavery* (Kingston, Jamaica, 1973), p. 284; Edward Brathwaite, *The Development of Creole Society in Jamaica 1770–1820* (Oxford: Clarendon Press, 1971).

2. In this chapter great care has been taken to use only seventeenth-century sources: *The Laws of Jamaica* (London, 1683); Sir Hans Sloane, *A Voyage to the Islands Madera, Barbados . . . and Jamaica*, 2 vols. (London, 1707, 1725); John Taylor, "The Present State of Jamaica" (1686: manuscript in the National Library of Jamaica; cited as "Taylor"); and the naval logs in the Public Record Office ("PRO"), London.

3. See S. A. G. Taylor, *The Western Design: An Account of Cromwell's Expedition to the Caribbean* (Kingston, Jamaica, 1965), pp. 1–37; and Carl Bridenbaugh and Roberta Bridenbaugh, *No Peace beyond the Line: The English in the Caribbean, 1624–1690* (New York: Oxford University Press, 1972), p. 30.

4. As Taylor explains in *Western Design*, other Maroon bands continued to live in the hills and eventually formed the origin of the Windward and Leeward Maroons of later times.

5. Sloane, *Voyage to the Islands*, preface to volume 1, n.p.

6. This could be judged by the names of the early landowners around Annotto Bay, preserved among the survey maps of the National Library of Jamaica.

7. See the entries in "Edward D'Oyley's Journal," ed. F. J. Osborne and S. A. G. Taylor, *Jamaican Historical Review* 10 (1973): 33–110; PRO Adm 51/345, log of H.M.S. *Falcon*, March 17, 1686, "42 pounds of rotten cheeze thrown overboard"; and Taylor, p. 189, which makes clear that butter and cheese were by no means West African staples.

8. See PRO Adm 51/3870, log of H.M.S. *Hunter*, June 12, 1676.

9. Bridenbaugh and Bridenbaugh, *No Peace beyond the Line*, p. 50; Sloane, *Voyage to the Islands*, p. xxviii.

10. Sloane, *Voyage to the Islands*, p. xviii.

11. Ibid., p. xix.

12. Richard Ligon, *A True and Exact History of the Island of Barbadoes* (London, 1673), p. 31.

13. Sloane, *Voyage to the Islands*, p. xix.

14. Bridenbaugh and Bridenbaugh, *No Peace beyond the Line*, p. 51.

15. Ibid., p. 50.

16. *Laws of Jamaica*, pp. 1–5.

17. Sloane, *Voyage to the Islands*, p. xvi; Taylor, pp. 338, 369. The term "escovitching" came from the Spanish *escabeche*, a pickle for fish.

18. Sloane, *Voyage to the Islands*, p. xxvii; Taylor, p. 72; Sloane, *Voyage to the Islands*, pp. xviii, xx; Taylor, pp. 403, 190.

19. Taylor, p. 395.
20. See James Hakewill, *A Picturesque Tour of the Island of Jamaica* (London, 1825); and Joseph Bartholomew Kidd, *Views of Jamaica*, 2 vols. (London, 1837).
21. Sloane, *Voyage to the Islands*, p. xlvii.
22. Taylor, p. 504.
23. Michael Pawson and David Buisseret, *Port Royal, Jamaica* (Oxford: Clarendon Press, 1975), pp. 109–10.
24. Sloane, *Voyage to the Islands*, p. xlvii.
25. Quoted by Bridenbaugh and Bridenbaugh, *No Peace beyond the Line*, p. 371.
26. Taylor, p. 264.
27. Others may be seen at Stokesfield and perhaps at Colbeck Castle.
28. One of the finest examples of early French creole architecture is the Pierre Menard Home, built in 1802 by slaves belonging to Menard, the first lieutenant governor of Illinois. The home is located near Chester, in southern Illinois. See figure 2.
29. Michael Pawson did publish the inventory of Thomas Freeman in the *Bulletin* of the Jamaican Historical Society.
30. Sloane, *Voyage to the Islands*, pp. xxx, xxi.
31. Ibid., pp. xcix, cxxvii, cxli.
32. Ibid., p. xxiv.
33. Richard Sheridan, in *Doctors and Slaves* (Cambridge, New York: Cambridge University Press, 1985), tends to play down these reciprocal influences.
34. Taylor, p. 547.
35. Frederic Cassidy, *Jamaica Talk* (London: Macmillan, 1961), p. 21.
36. Ibid., pp. 391–406.
37. Richard Rath, "African Music in Seventeenth-Century Jamaica: Cultural Transit and Transition," *William and Mary Quarterly* 50 (1993): 700–26; see pp. 707, 725.
38. Richard Blome, *A Description of the Island of Jamaica* (London, 1672), p. 42.
39. Taylor, p. 563.
40. Ibid., p. 575.
41. See Trevor Burnard, "European Migration to Jamaica, 1655–1780," *William and Mary Quarterly* 33 (1996): 769–96.
42. Agnes Whitson, *The Constitutional Development of Jamaica 1660–1729* (Manchester: University Press, 1929), p. 48.
43. Ibid., p. 142.

"The Facility Offered by the Country"

Daniel H. Usner, Jr.

The Creolization of Agriculture in the Lower Mississippi Valley

The concept of creolization, which originated in the study of languages, characterizes the process of interaction among different cultural groups in a colonial region as they adapted to a new environment.[1] In the eighteenth-century Lower Mississippi Valley, responses of both American Indian and colonial peoples to each other and to the land and its resources generated the development of cultural practices that became deeply rooted in the region. Patterns of intercultural exchange, adoption, and fusion in the realm of livelihood were especially influenced by the natural environment of the Lower Mississippi Valley and by the particular sequence of peoples migrating into the region. The creolization of agriculture resulted from this ongoing mixture of different subsistence traditions, with a heavy American Indian impact, as natives and newcomers alike adapted to changing economic circumstances.[2]

Whenever discussing creolization in the Lower Mississippi Valley one must mention the confused and politicized meaning of the word "creole" in this region. Scattered documents from the eighteenth century indicate that it was originally used in Louisiana mainly as an adjective to designate settlers and slaves born in the colony, distinguishing them from people who migrated from Europe, Africa, or any other outside region. By the nineteenth century the word took on multiple and conflicting meanings. Used broadly at the beginning of that century to distinguish native-born, French-speaking Louisianians from English-speaking Americans moving into the Lower Mississippi Valley, "creole" was eventually appropriated by upper-class white Louisianians to designate the descendants of French and Spanish colonists. Although the intent, especially after the Civil War, was to exclude people of color from the identity, many Louisianians of African descent never abandoned the ascription.[3]

Throughout this linguistically and racially polarizing contest over identity, however, people in south Louisiana continued to apply the original meaning of the word "creole" to plants and animals bred within the region. Hand-printed signs reading "creole tomatoes," "creole onions," and "creole garlic" are still common sights at local produce stands, where buyers and sellers routinely acclaim the superiority of regionally grown vegetables and fruits. And, of course, there is the familiar, yet mysterious cuisine called Creole. As a style of cooking it is often associated with New Orleans high society, although its evolution is more broadly based.[4] This persistent usage of "creole" in food markets and kitchens to the present day provides an important clue to the value of applying the analytical concept of creolization to the evolution of agriculture in the Lower Mississippi Valley, not only for the formative years of the eighteenth century but for migrations and adaptations during subsequent times as well.

Because of the acquisition of local knowledge about how to produce food in the Lower Mississippi Valley and its evolution into creole subsistence practices, ordinary people in early Louisiana managed to maintain some control over their livelihoods in face of significant opposition from upper-class colonial interests. But in order to begin tracing this process, it is necessary to unravel the agricultural strategies deployed by most rural Louisianians from the value judgments imposed upon them by others. Officials, merchants, and planters sought to develop commercial agriculture that would produce export crops for the transatlantic market. Land and labor were channeled by these groups in ways that threatened the autonomy and flexibility that settlers and slaves found in creolized farming, hunting, and trading practices. But even as more and more inhabitants of the Lower Mississippi Valley became willing or unwilling participants in the export economy, people attempted to minimize their dependency upon it. Small-scale farming and herding, along with other subsistence activities devised during early years of colonization, allowed Louisianians to secure a measure of economic independence in face of mounting market pressures.

Creolization of agriculture created in rural Louisiana what some scholars call a moral economy or subsistence ethic. As did their counterparts in other regions around the world, poor farmers and slaves in the Lower Mississippi Valley improvised ways of protecting household needs and traditional values against the destabilizing effects and disadvantageous circumstances of commercial production.[5] Although there is much disagreement over how best to characterize this behavior, current scholarship reveals that agrarian societies in America are better understood as spatial mixes of activities at varying degrees of dependency upon commercial markets than as temporal sequences of evolutionary stages of production. In some of the most export-oriented economic settings many farmers maintained self-sufficiency as their priority and participated in the market economy with great caution.[6] Even on large-scale plantations slaves planted food crops and garden vegetables and raised chickens and pigs for home consumption and local markets. Across the American South, especially during the colonial period, few plantations were strictly monocrop operations or were isolated from smaller mixed-crop farms.[7]

This essay weaves together an analysis of creolized agriculture between the opposing perspectives of its practitioners and its critics in order to demonstrate a need to filter descriptions of subsistence activities from the heavy judgments of antagonistic observers. A better understanding of how plantation society physically enveloped and ideologically marginalized the everyday strategies of rural folk is the main objective. As will be documented over several generations, local gentry and outside observers tended to downplay the knowledge and resourcefulness behind creole livelihood by exaggerating the indolence of small-farm owners and inflating the natural bounty of their environments. In the words of a French governor in 1764, "The facility offered by the country to live on its natural productions has created habits of laziness."[8] This misrepresentation of Louisiana inhabitants as too easily enjoying nature's abundance would be repeated again and again by self-serving observers, and for too long it excluded the ordinary settler's interests and practices from careful examination. Instead, many historians have minimized the embeddedness and persistence of the subsistence ethic by portraying it as a passing, and even primitive, phase in the development of agriculture and commerce. The powerful nationalist image of hunters, traders, herders, and farmers moving westward in succession further prevented historians from recognizing the complicated and long-term coexistence of different patterns of agriculture in many North American regions.

The specific mixture of subsistence activities supporting livelihood across the Lower Mississippi Valley during the eighteenth century originated in the woodland economy developed by American Indian villagers over previous centuries. The relative importance of particular means of production such as farming or fishing varied from tribe to tribe, depending upon the ecological niche occupied by the group. Life in the floodplain of the Mississippi River revolved more heavily around the seasonal procurement of abundant fish, mammals, and wild plants available in lowland forests and waters, whereas people living on upland terraces or in the hilly country devoted more of their subsistence cycle to planting corn, beans, and other domestic plants on fertile ground. Across the region, however, Indians had created village economies that efficiently exploited a wide range of resources. In the alluvial lowlands Indian villages occupied natural levees, where inhabitants cultivated crops on narrow fields during the summer months and procured a variety of nuts, berries, and small mammals into the fall seasons. Over the winter months Indians dispersed into camps along lakes and bayous in order to exploit deer, bear, fish, and waterfowl. With springtimes marked by rising water levels on the rivers, Indians returned to their villages situated on protected natural levees or bluffs. Here they concentrated on deer and other animals driven upland by flooding and on spring-ripening fruits such as mayhaws (a hawthorn of the southern United States) and blackberries.[9]

Once the rivers began to recede from their banks, Indians shifted their attention to agriculture by late spring. In order to start new fields in forested lowlands they had to clear thick patches of cane and sometimes remove oak and cypress trees before planting their crops. Cutting and burning proved to be effective methods of removal. Antoine Le Page du Pratz observed Indian farmers cutting the canes in early March and peeling rings of several feet of bark off the bases of the trees, "as then the sap is in motion in that country." Two weeks later when the dry canes were set afire, "the sap of the trees are thereby made to descend, and the branches are burnt, which kills the trees." Fields prepared in this way acquired high fertility without much labor and without animal fertilizers. The seeds of corn were sown directly into the nutritive ashes of burnt wood and cane. "Such as begin a plantation in the woods, thick with cane," noted Le Page du Pratz, "have an advantage in the maiz, that makes amends for the labor of clearing the ground."[10] This system of agriculture, however, required that bottomland fields be left fallow after several harvest seasons for new vegetation to grow. What were impenetrable canebrakes one decade became productive fields the next, and vice versa. The actual longevity of Indian fields remains uncertain, but the periodic relocation of fields in lowland forests probably contributed to some of the change in village locations during the eighteenth century.[11]

Settlers and slaves in colonial Louisiana borrowed forms of production long used by Lower Mississippi Valley Indians mainly because such a mixture of farming, hunting, fishing, and gathering protected them from the environmental and economic uncertainties of living in a strange land. Cultivation of food plants that worked for Indians, on small plots of bottomland, secured a livelihood for most colonial inhabitants. Few farmers could afford to devote all of their agricultural production to export crops such as tobacco and indigo. At best they sought a balance between commercial and subsistence farming. Even on the largest plantations slaves spent much of their time producing their own food sources. Settlers and slaves also pursued wild plants and animals in neighboring forests and waters in order to round out their diets. Sometimes a flood, drought, or a hurricane wiped out colonial and Indian fields, making alternative sources of food essential.[12]

Most settlers in the Lower Mississippi Valley cultivated a mixture of food crops, especially corn and rice, on farms of fewer than 200 acres. During the 1720s small farms called *habitations* gradually spread along the banks of the Mississippi between the New Orleans area and the settlement of Pointe Coupée. In order to keep colonists there and to encourage agriculture, the Company of the Indies offered settlers moderately sized tracts of free land, usually with 5 arpents of river frontage and 40 arpents deep from the bank (200 arpents, or 170 acres). "A man with his wife or his partner," wrote Father Paul Du Poisson in 1727, "clears a little ground, builds himself a house of four piles, covers it with sheets of bark, and plants corn and rice for his provisions; the next year he raises a little more for food, and has also a field of tobacco; if at last he succeeds in having three or four Negroes, then he is out of his difficulties." Resembling a village of sorts, neighboring farms composed a single settlement or district.[13] Ordinances prohibiting speculation and providing free concessions during the French period did not completely prevent land monopolization, but they did ease the process of settlement for many propertyless immigrants. This pattern of long, thin grants of land stretching back from frontage on the river and averaging fewer than two hundred acres was adopted by Spain and Great Britain in their later efforts to colonize the region with families of farmers. Each farmer received a grant of land on the Mississippi or some other waterway and was obliged to cultivate the soil within a year and to maintain a levee to control flooding.[14]

Occupation of Indian fields and employment of Indian laborers by early settlers also contributed to continuity between native and colonial farming in early Louisiana. Abandoned native villages became prime sites for the location of concessions granted by the Company of the Indies. Previously cleared areas appropriated by Europeans in colonial North America were known to the English as "Indian old fields" and to the French as "vieux villages." In Louisiana they included both scattered fields left fallow by Indian cultivators and entire town sites deserted because of epidemics, wars, or migrations. The concession granted to Paris Duvernay was located about seventy miles above New Orleans at the old village of the Bayogoulas. Situated seven or eight arpents west of the riverbank of the Mississippi and relatively safe from flooding, this site contained, according to a company official, "two hundred and fifty arpents of land in which the plough may pass everywhere." Ten miles downriver most of the German families transported to Louisiana by the company "settled on very good land where there were formerly Indian fields easy to cultivate."[15] In some cases individual settlers and soldiers purchased parcels of farmland directly from Indian villagers in order to begin planting their own crops more easily. Rarely were Indian lands coerced from them, but Indian labor was expropriated through warfare. Between 1708 and 1722 the number of Indian slaves working on Louisiana farms increased from 80 to 169. These men and women undoubtedly showed Europeans and Africans working beside them some useful techniques for raising food.[16]

Official efforts to expand commercial agriculture clashed repeatedly with means of livelihood preferred by common settlers in the Lower Mississippi Valley. Early colonial inhabitants showed little eagerness to commit themselves to planting commercial crops, frustrating the hopes of colonial planners and investors for developing an export economy. During the 1720s the Company of the Indies promoted tobacco production through a series of measures: sending experienced tobacco workers and African slaves to the colony, paying artificially high prices for the harvests, and even offering bounties to concession directors who chose to plant the crop.[17] But few settlers could afford to purchase slaves, even on credit, from the company. Trade with local Indians and production of their own food required less labor and land. Many of the several thousand African slaves shipped to the colony for commercial production also turned to small-scale farming and trading to mitigate their bondage in America.

Gradually an increasing number of *petits habitants* committed their farms to the production of export crops, especially if they managed to purchase a few slaves. They and a small number of wealthier planters introduced new forms of production to the Lower Mississippi Valley—operations geared toward producing larger quantities of tobacco, indigo, and other commodities for the Atlantic market. In addition to the financial shortcomings suffered as producers in one of France's marginal colonies, Louisiana planters specializing in commercial crops faced the environmental hazards of heavy rains and floods, hurricanes, and periodic droughts. Excessive rain during the summer of 1728 ruined most of Louisiana's tobacco crop, including twenty thousand pounds owned by Gov. Étienne Boucher de Périer, who joked bitterly, "I did not at first feel my loss because I thought that the deluge of water that we have experienced for fifty days would carry me away after my tobacco." Just two years later a severely dry season prevented the governor and others from even planting tobacco, and then in 1732 three-fourths of the tobacco seed from a successful harvest was destroyed by a hurricane that struck on August 29. With planting delayed in the spring of 1734 by three months of flooding, Louisiana officials prematurely lamented: "This country is subject to such great vicissitude that one can almost not count on the crops at all. Now there is too much drought, now too much rain." Levees and canals were constructed in time and allowed tobacco and indigo producers to withstand seasonal risks, but exportation of commercial crops from the Lower Mississippi Valley remained erratic until the end of the eighteenth century.[18]

Even on Louisiana farms inextricably tied to the Atlantic market, settlers and slaves combined subsistence with commercial activities into a seasonal cycle of production. They realized that the surest way to minimize personal risk in the Lower Mississippi Valley was to utilize the region's variety of food sources as they became seasonally available. Farmers supplemented their diets with game, fish, and other wild foods taken from local forests and waters. Slaves hunted, fished, and collected edible plants for their own use, for their owners' kitchens, and for the regional food markets.[19] Philippe Haynault's farm at Pointe Coupée was a typical unit of agricultural production for the mid–eighteenth century, in which daily economic life revolved around the production of food and tobacco. At his death in 1743 Haynault owned 280 arpents of land, six cattle, seven hogs, and ten chickens, along with two horses owned jointly with another farmer. His labor force consisted of two African men, an Indian woman and her daughter—all slaves—and a white overseer. Haynault lived in a cypress-shingled house thirty by fourteen feet, built on posts, while his slaves inhabited separate huts. Food provisions stored on the farm included twenty-four barrels of corn, two barrels of beans, and a barrel of Illinois flour. Among Haynault's personal possessions were six Indian pots and three Indian sifters. The Indian women probably took care of the corn and bean crops, with some assistance from the other slaves at planting and harvesting time, and she undoubtedly prepared meals for the farm's residents with some of her traditional cookware. When not busy with planting, replanting, weeding, and drying tobacco, the men spent much of their time tending the livestock and hunting for wild game.[20]

Slaves living on large plantations probably exerted greater control over production of food. Those on smaller farms, like that of Haynault, lived under tighter supervision by owners who often worked alongside them in the fields. But on the indigo plantations around New Orleans slaves were allowed to cultivate their own gardens, raise their own poultry, and even market their produce. In 1738 the concession of Chaouachas, located about fifteen miles below New Orleans on the west bank of the Mississippi River, housed 153 slaves who produced large quantities of rice, tobacco, and indigo and raised a herd of seventy cattle for the owner-investors in Paris. Comprising forty different nuclear families, these people lived in twenty separate cabins upriver from the manager's house and the plantation fields of rice, tobacco, and indigo. Behind their quarters, "surrounded by stakes, roofed by Palmetto" like a distinct village, were fields on which the slave families cultivated their own food. The short distance from New Orleans made it easy for slaves from Chaouachas to market their goods in town on weekends.[21]

The independent production and marketing of crops by Louisiana slaves resulted from both their own desire to cultivate familiar goods and the economic interests of their owners. Managing the Company of the Indies plantation across the river from New Orleans between 1726 and 1734, Le Page du Pratz recognized the inclination among slaves to satisfy personally their own subsistence needs and eating tastes. He recommended that owners give "a small piece of waste ground" to their slaves, "engage them to cultivate it for their own profit," and purchase their produce upon fair and just terms.[22] Planters thereby acquired goods to sell to other colonists, although the slaves preferred direct participation in the marketplace. Small-scale cultivating and marketing of foodstuffs by slaves had several advantages in Louisiana, as in other plantation colonies. They helped owners maintain slaves at a level of subsistence minimizing hardship, death, and rebellion; provided consumers with a larger quantity and wider array of foods than would otherwise have been available; and gained for slaves some measure of autonomy from their masters. Colonial officials intermittently enforced regulations upon slave peddlers, requiring them by 1751 to carry written permits from their owners, but the open marketing of goods by slaves benefited too many people for the prohibition against it to be enforced before the last quarter of the century.[23]

In time colonial farmers from the surrounding countryside brought grains, vegetables, fruits, poultry, and game to the multiethnic market at New Orleans. German immigrants who settled above the city during the 1720s became notable food provisioners. "They bring every day to the market," observed one contemporary, "all kinds of produce to the city." When raids by Choctaw Indians caused families to flee from the German coast to the city in 1748, New Orleans became, as Gov. Philippe de Rigault de Vaudreuil reported, "deprived of the comforts that those settlers provided for it by their industry and their thrift."²⁴ Thomas Jefferys later called the Germans "the purveyors of the capital, whither they bring, weekly, cabbages, salads, fruits, greens, and pulse of all sorts, as well as vast quantities of wildfowl, salt pork, and many excellent sorts of fish."²⁵ Other groups of independent farmers also marketed foodstuffs in the city. French, free black, and American Indian families provisioned New Orleans from their own gardens and fields. During the 1760s newly arriving Acadian and Canary Island settlers began to plant corn, rice, and other food crops and became important producers in the local food market.²⁶

Jean Romel's and Pierre Arcenaux's farms represented typical operations along the Mississippi River just above New Orleans. By the late 1760s descendants of German immigrants and newly arrived Acadians numbered just over two hundred families in the parishes of Saint Charles and Saint John. Although the total population of 1,744 included 764 slaves, most of these families owned no slaves. The agricultural production for all farms in Saint Charles and Saint John Parishes, according to the 1770 census, totaled 18,924 quarts of corn, 6,796 quarts of rice, and 202 quarts of beans. In 1766 with his wife and four children Romel owned six arpents of river frontage, thirteen cattle, five pigs, and four horses. Pierre Arcenaux's family in 1769 included his wife and five children, and on their six arpents of frontage they possessed nine cattle, twelve pigs, and three horses. During the 1770s small-scale farming expanded down Bayou Lafourche as Acadian settlers acquired available lands west of the Mississippi River. Among the eighty-four households counted there in 1777, the Charles Prejean and François Duhan families were representative. Prejean raised fourteen cattle, four pigs, two sheep, and three horses on six arpents of frontage, while Duhan's seven-arpent frontage held nine cattle, three pigs, and two horses.²⁷

The multiple roles played by Indians, settlers, and slaves in the creolization of agriculture in the Lower Mississippi Valley channeled various cultural influences into the regional diet. Culinary tastes and cooking techniques were undoubtedly shaped by the combination of food sources pursued by different ethnic groups in this rich natural environment. No exact lines or precise moments of influence can be delineated, but the origins of Louisiana's legendary creole cuisine lie in the creolization of agriculture and other cross-cultural changes in livelihood that occurred over the eighteenth century. The most extensive influence upon diet was, of course, American Indian uses of corn. Settlers and slaves not only adopted maize as a food crop but learned from Indians various ways of preparing it for consumption. A previous knowledge of cultivating and cooking maize helped African slaves adapt to American Indian horticulture and facilitated, in the long run, the persistence of some distinct features of the Indian diet in Lower Mississippi Valley foodways. People in the Upper Guinea region of West Africa, where a vast majority of Louisiana's slaves originated in the eighteenth century, were generally more familiar with maize than were their European contemporaries. Introduced to West Africa by Portuguese traders in the sixteenth century, American corn served as a major food source for the slave trade and quickly entered the cuisine of some societies in present-day Nigeria and Dahomey.[28]

West African knowledge of rice further creolized agriculture and diversified the diets of colonial Louisianians. In 1718 the Company of the Indies instructed the captains of two slave ships bound for Louisiana to buy at least a few Africans "who know how to cultivate rice" as well as some "hogsheads of rice suitable for planting." Whereas Indian or colonial farms often had to wait for the waters to retreat from their fields before planting corn, rice could be sown before the rivers overflowed every spring and promised, therefore, to protect the colony from delayed or deficient grain supplies. Slaves in Louisiana, most of them from the Senegal River region, soon were planting rice along the seasonally flooded banks of the Mississippi. By 1724 slave owners in Louisiana had begun to pay their debts to the company with rice, realizing the hope of colonial planners for a new export commodity. More important for the development of the local economy, rice quickly became a major domestic food for settlers and slaves alike. Gov. Jean-Baptiste Le Moyne de Bienville reported in 1726, "I admit that this is not a great return for France but it is a great comfort for the colony and it will be the riches of the little settlers. . . . There are no bad years for rice after what we have seen these last three years."[29]

The strong linkage of farming with hunting, fishing, gathering, and herding in the subsistence economy of eighteenth-century Louisiana allowed Indians, settlers, and slaves to mix domestic and wild food sources into a creolized diet. Less visible than the food crops, livestock, fish, and game exchanged at marketplaces were the meals prepared inside colonial households. Uncertain etymologies befuddle efforts to trace definite origins, but some characteristic dishes of Louisiana creole culture represent the cross-cultural influences that originated during the eighteenth century. The thick base, or roux, from which all forms of gumbo are made is produced either by cooking sliced okra in slowly heated oil or by adding powdered sassafras toward the end of cooking. The name of the finished stock of seafood, poultry, meat, or any combination of these ingredients has been attributed to the Angolan word for okra, *guingombo*, a vegetable brought to the region by African slaves, or to the Choctaw word for sassafras powder, *kombo ashish*, which local Indians continued to market into the twentieth century. The elusive origins of another spicy, rice-based dish, jambalaya, have led one folklorist to suggest that a creolization of the French *jambon*, "ham," and the Choctaw *falaya*, "long," went into naming this meat-stretching meal.[30]

Later immigrants to the Lower Mississippi Valley eagerly took advantage of subsistence and exchange practices already discovered and developed by creole inhabitants. Reporting on the arrival of some two hundred Acadians in September, 1766, Louisiana's first Spanish governor minimized the returns that one should expect from the money spent to assist their passage: "They are not able to cultivate indigo nor tobacco without having first a competent number of negroes to do the work and they will be reduced to owning a few animals and to cultivating grains and roots for their own consumption, with which they will be rich as far as they are personally concerned but will not enrich the colony nor contribute to the growth of its commerce, because it will never get beyond producing wood, indigo of very poor quality, and tobacco in small quantities and of ordinary quality."[31] Officials might have lowered their expectations of most newcomers, but the governments of both Spanish Louisiana and British West Florida still offered immigrants small parcels of free acreage along the Lower Mississippi Valley's waterways in order to stimulate population growth. By continuing this French land policy, later colonial authorities actually fostered the spread of creolized agriculture.[32]

In order to accelerate the expansion of cotton and sugar agriculture in the Lower Mississippi Valley after the 1763 Treaty of Paris, however, the colonial governments of both West Florida and Louisiana made much larger landholdings available to slave-owning immigrants. Consequently, tension between land-hungry planters and small-scale farmers steadily escalated toward the end of the eighteenth century. This process continued under United States administration since the federal government's land policy did little to deter the accumulation of large landholdings during the early nineteenth century. Wealthy planters eventually owned most of the fertile land along rivers and bayous in the Lower Mississippi Valley. Creole agriculture operations now had to be conducted in a variegated landscape containing small-scale and large-scale farms on limited or remote spaces on the edge of plantation production. Small farms often consisted of crops planted on narrow ridges and levees surrounded by cotton or sugar plantations. Many families that had been farming along the Mississippi River for years now migrated to tributary bayous and backcountry waterways, duplicating eighteenth-century practices on new lands. New migrants from eastern parts of the United States clustered in the upland pine woods, still in proximity to plantations in the alluvial valleys but secure against planter domination for the time being.[33]

Throughout this period of agrarian transformation, observers whose values favored rapid commercialization of agriculture routinely moralized about the inferiority of creolized farming. After describing in detail how to plant, weed, and harvest corn, English naturalist and cartographer Bernard Romans remarked in the mid 1770s: "A Report has been spread that on the Mississippi it was only necessary to burn the canes, make a hole in the ground and put the grain in, and it will grow without culture; It is true, but less wise men than Solomon will know such a field at sight to be that of the sluggard, and know the owner by his shabby appearance."[34] Major Amos Stoddard saw "the character of the French people" in behavior that he considered indolent, yet honest. "They obtain but little," the United States military officer observed about Mississippi Valley inhabitants, "and little satisfies their desires. They usually live within their incomes, and are never so uneasy as when in debt."[35] An early nineteenth-century French traveler, Charles Robin, painted a more sympathetic picture of the moral economy practiced by Acadian farmers upriver from New Orleans, capturing the special relationship between their natural environment and their subsistence activities:

> Twenty leagues above the city the Acadian coast begins and runs about another twenty up from there. Like the Germans they work their own farms. Only a few of them have Negroes. Already the population has risen so that the farms are sub-divided into strips of two or three arpents of frontage. You must remember that each plot ran back forty arpents from the river. Only about half that depth, however, is under cultivation, the rest being inundated and covered with cypress and similar swamp vegetation.
>
> Rice, corn, several kinds of beans, melons (in season), pumpkin, salted pork and beef make up their principal diet. The customs can be compared to those of our farmers of Beauce and Brie. . . . They do not show the zeal in their work that their European confreres would, for on the one hand, they are not pressed by necessity, and on the other hand, the lack of outlets for their product discourages them from greater efforts. However, they are still Frenchmen, passionately loving their country, proud to work for it, and showing a great predilection for its products.[36]

Seargent Prentiss, a transplanted New Englander living in Natchez, traveled with a friend down Bayou Lafourche during March, 1829. He noticed how this part of Louisiana was just beginning to be settled by Americans now that "it was found to contain the best sugar lands in the United States, and perhaps in the world." Observing that "it has, however, been settled for some time, by the French—and even at present, they form at least nine-tenths of the population," Prentiss offered a typical judgment: "They are the poorest, most ignorant, set of beings you ever saw—without the least enterprise or industry. They raise only a little corn and a few sweet potatoes—merely sufficient to support life; yet they seem perfectly contented and happy, and have balls almost every day—I attended one, and was invited to several others." Contributing to the emerging stereotype of Louisiana Cajuns, Prentiss nonetheless discerned inadvertently how the environment both facilitated and warranted the kind of agriculture that he disparaged. He wrote that along each of the many bayous paralleling the Mississippi River "is a high land, from one to ten acres in depth, on either side, after which it falls into a swamp, and so continued till you come to another bayou; Thus, between every two bayous there is an extensive swamp."³⁷

The challenging adaptation to the wetlands environment of south Louisiana, so easily dismissed by Prentiss and others during the early nineteenth century, was mainly carried out by first- and second-generation Acadian and Canary Island settlers whose migration to the region had occurred under Spanish dominion. Slave-owning planters perceived the economic practices of Acadian farmers as a threat to their cotton and sugar operations for a few reasons. First, there was the familiar concern over controlling enslaved workers who could readily participate in a shadow economy of small-scale production and exchange. With the slave population rapidly increasing and plantations becoming larger in scale, this apprehension over slaves' interaction with non–slave owners grew more intense. Then there was, of course, increasing pressure for land along the Mississippi and other major waterways as more and more aspiring planters migrated into the region. And because most of these newcomers were Anglo-Americans from other parts of the United States, antagonism toward the culture of French-speaking Louisianians further galvanized condemnation of their livelihood. Acadian responses to these hostile forces, however, perpetuated the creolization of agriculture in south Louisiana. Migrating to more remote areas in order to maintain some autonomy in their subsistence and to secure enough land for their children, the people who would become known as Cajuns relied heavily on the traditional combination of seasonal activities. Like the Chitimachas, Houmas, and other American Indians, whose collective population had dwindled to a small number in the area by then, Acadian settlers raised small quantities of food crops on natural levees and foraged for wild food sources in the still-bountiful wetlands. Many planted some cotton or sugar alongside their corn, beans, and sweet potatoes. Others herded cattle and other livestock on the prairies west of Bayou Teche. As the plantation economy continued to expand around their settlements, Cajuns increasingly turned to day labor and commercial fishing as supplementary sources of income.³⁸

The Canary Islanders who settled in several different communities in south Louisiana adapted similarly to their new environment under the same circumstances. Early in the nineteenth century Thomas Ashe visited the Saint Bernardo settlement at Terre-aux-Boeufs. On narrow strips of land along the bayou, with marshes on both sides, the Isleños—as Ashe predictably phrased it—"content themselves with raising fowls, corn, and vegetables, for the market of New Orleans." Over the years the Isleños maintained a secure livelihood by producing garden crops, livestock, and seafood for the nearby urban market. But as Ashe noted about other settlements in the area, there seemed to be little dependence upon a particular marketplace since "every settler provides his own family." Again an outsider simply assumed that the ease of subsistence in a lush environment discouraged participation in the mainstream economy: "His grounds abound with stock; the woods with game; and the river with fish; where is the necessity of a market?" Social and economic motivations for an Isleños strategy of maintaining a measure of independence from the plantation system do not seem to have crossed the English traveler's mind.[39]

Many Anglo-American settlers moving into the Lower Mississippi Valley during the nineteenth century, mainly from other parts of the South, also adapted to the host society by finding an early economic niche in small-scale agriculture. Their participation in the cotton economy was supplemented by raising livestock, growing food crops, and hunting game. As described by Timothy Flint, principal of the Seminary of Rapide, the narrow stream bottomlands that crisscrossed the upland pine woods of Louisiana "will bring three or four crops of corn without manure, and are admirable for the sweet potato." He reported that on both sides of the Red River settlers "generally support themselves by raising cattle, which they number by hundreds." Flint concluded that "nothing can be easier than subsistence in the pine woods. There being little call for labour, the inhabitants labour little, and are content with indolence, health, and poverty."[40] In the 1830s Joseph Holt Ingraham encountered a group of farmers visiting the Mississippi River town of Natchez. As he described the scene, "Seated in a circle around their bread and cheese, were half a dozen as rough, rude, honest-looking countrymen from the back part of the state, as you could find in the nursery of New-England's yeomanry." Describing how these Mississippi yeomen camped inside a circle formed by their carts, instead of staying in city taverns, Ingraham succinctly characterized their position in the regional economy: "They are small farmers—own a few negroes—cultivate a small tract of land, and raise a few bales of cotton, which they bring to market themselves."[41]

Slaves working on newly created plantations in early-nineteenth-century Louisiana also turned to the environment's wide variety of food sources in order to secure some diversity and autonomy in their livelihood. Describing in 1823 how 175 slaves were clearing land and constructing buildings on her husband's new plantation along Bayou Grosse Tete in Iberville Parish, Caroline Bell reported that "the negroes . . . prefer the Bayou infinitely to the [Mississippi] River." There they could find "the greatest abundance of game, plenty of the finest Fish—good clear water, which is a great luxury to them—and indeed will be to us also."[42] The old pattern of adaptation, in which slaves combined seasonal subsistence activities with commercial production on the plantation, was thus reinforced by African American newcomers to the Lower Mississippi Valley. Solomon Northrup, a New Yorker who was kidnapped and sold into slavery in 1841, described how slaves in the lower Red River Valley supplemented their weekly rations by hunting in the swamps for raccoons and opossums. This had to be done at night on their own free time and with clubs and dogs, since slaves were not allowed to use guns. Driven to invention by the exhausting effects of this nocturnal pursuit of meat after a long day of plantation work, Northrup designed his own fish trap in order to obtain much-needed food from a bayou near his cabin.[43] Wherever permitted by their owners, slaves continued to rely upon their own gardens, poultry, and hogs for both household subsistence and local exchange. At the Houmas plantation of John Burnside, William Russell observed that "on the borders of the forest the negroes are allowed to plant corn for their own use, and sometimes they have an overplus, which they sell to their masters." He also noted that behind their cabins "are rude poultry-hutches, which with geese and turkeys and a few pigs, form the perquisites of the slaves, and the sole source from which they derive their acquaintance with currency."[44]

As space along the Mississippi River became more and more constricted for small-scale farmers, their relationships with neighboring planters remained tense. Creolized agriculture, surrounded by expanding cotton and sugar plantations, represented a threat to the security and prosperity of slave owners committed more than ever to single-crop operations. In 1853–54 Frederick

Law Olmsted noticed at the corner of a large sugar plantation "a hamlet consisting of about a dozen small houses or huts, built of wood or clay, in the old French peasant style." The residents of this community raised corn and rice, but Olmsted's host "described them as lazy vagabonds, doing but little work, and spending much time in shooting, fishing, and play." The sugar planter had already bought land from some of his neighbors and hoped eventually to move all of them away even at the expense of paying twice or thrice the actual value of their property. Olmsted reported, "As fast as he got possession, he destroyed their houses and gardens, removed their fences and trees, and brought all their land into his cane-plantation." Olmsted learned that this planter's predatory behavior was probably driven more by his powerful animosity toward the small-farm owners than by the opportunity to expand his own production. He accused them of demoralizing his slaves, as explained to Olmsted in some detail:

> Seeing them living in apparent comfort, without much property and without steady labour, the slaves could not help thinking that it was unnecessary for men to work so hard as they themselves were obliged to, and that if they were free they would not work. Besides, the intercourse of these people with the negroes was not favourable to good discipline. They would get the negroes to do them little services, and would pay with luxuries which he did not wish his slaves to have. It was better that they never saw anybody off their own plantation; they should, if possible, have no intercourse with any other white men than their owner or overseer; especially, it was desirable that they should not see white men who did not command their respect, and whom they did not always feel to be superior to themselves, and able to command them.[45]

This familiar complaint against independent farmers masked a far more complicated web of relations among slaves and slave owners in the Lower Mississippi Valley, which made a lasting impact on class and race in the region. Observing some antagonism between the owner of Orange Grove Plantation and a group of "small Creole planters" downriver, William Howard Russell suggested that interaction among Ascension Parish residents was quite incongruent. First of all, according to this London *Times* special correspondent, landowners were still tenaciously resisting efforts by their wealthier neighbors to buy them out with tempting prices, although subdivision of farms from generation to generation had slivered their estates into narrower and poorer operations. Some of these Mississippi River farmers also owned slaves, producing sugar as well as corn for the market, and had even earned a reputation for working them more harshly than did big-farm planters. "But it is also true," Russell noted, "that the slaves have closer relations with the families of their owners, and live in more intimate connection with them than they do under the strict police of the large plantations."[46] Under the intensifying pressure of more powerful planters, it became increasingly difficult for settlers to practice a mixture of economic activities on their diminishing lands—which included informal exchange relations with plantation slaves. Some small-farm owners demanded longer hours of labor from their slaves in order to compete in the cotton or sugar business, although sharing work and leisure involved personal interaction. The ongoing displacement of small-scale white producers from the banks of the Mississippi and adjacent bayous had, in the long run, an ambivalent effect on their relations with African Americans. Some families retreated to more remote lands, perhaps blaming slavery for their plight, while others turned to employment as plantation overseers or managers. An antagonism against wealthy planters, shared by poor white and black Louisianians, was overshadowed by a resentment over unequal roles and opportunities.[47]

Over the entire nineteenth century creole agriculture in the Lower Mississippi Valley became increasingly marginalized under a variety of old and new pressures. Already excluded from much of the region's naturally fertile lands, small-scale farmers witnessed additional acreage being transformed for plantation agriculture as wetlands were drained and levees were built at significant public expense. Hunting and gathering in bottomland habitats for household subsistence and local markets became more difficult to practice. Meanwhile, the production of cotton by small-farm owners in the piney hills country of Mississippi and northern Louisiana caused serious erosion of the soil, diminishing the productivity and increasing the vulnerability of their small-scale operations. Family succession of ordinary farmsteads along rivers and bayous also weakened their agrarian base, as original grants of land were cut lengthwise into narrower and narrower strips for heirs. After the Civil War tenancy and sharecropping became the lot of more and more farmers across the region. Many tenants struggled against mounting odds to produce enough food for their families as cotton became the sole means of paying rent and debts. Postemancipation terrorism and Jim Crow legislation aimed at African Americans demolished whatever remained from the customary network of interethnic exchange. Although many rural whites and blacks shared a deepening poverty by the 1930s, they were unable to rebuild an alternative moral economy that might have mitigated or overcome their common plight. The Mississippi River flood of 1927 and the Great Depression completely undermined the viability of independent farming in many places.[48] Many African American tenant farmers in the Mississippi Delta were still able to grow vegetables on small patches of ground and to raise hogs and poultry, in keeping with plantation practices since slavery. But with mechanization of cotton agriculture after World War II, more and more landowners prohibited their tenants from maintaining vegetable gardens, chicken coops, and livestock pens.[49]

Creolized economic practices, however, persisted in scattered pockets of the Lower Mississippi Valley. South Louisiana and other lowland areas remained especially supportive of small-scale farming mixed with hunting, fishing, and herding. Perhaps more than any other subregion, the banks of Bayou Lafourche represented this traditional livelihood well into the twentieth century. In 1881 the Louisiana state commissioner of immigration depicted the landscape as follows: "The plantations along [Bayou Lafourche] are generally laid out in large tracts (though there are many small ones), the front portion being appropriated to cane and corn, and the rear land to tenants who cultivate rice. In the rear of the plantations, which usually extend to eighty acres, are found dry bayous having high lands on each bank; these ridges are mostly occupied by small proprietors, who cultivate cane, corn, cotton, and rice, and such other crops as contribute to the comfort of their homes and the support of their families."[50] Nearly sixty years later a typical farm along Bayou Lafourche was described as having eight arpents planted in sugarcane, eight arpents in corn and peas, and two arpents in potatoes, onions, and other vegetables. This combination of food and cash crops attained for many rural households a degree of security with minimal risk. As an elderly Acadian farmer told cultural geographer Lauren Post, "a crop of two bales of cotton was too small; a crop of four bales was too much work; a crop of three bales was 'just right.'"[51] Italians and Yugoslavs settling in and around New Orleans toward the end of the nineteenth century became prominent participants in the local food market and thereby duplicated some practices of earlier migrants.[52] Ethnic groups entering the region even during this century, especially the Vietnamese, have perpetuated to some extent this creolization of livelihood by adapting their traditional means of production and exchange to economic and environmental conditions.[53]

Forms of livelihood shaped by creolization of agriculture continued to be undervalued by outside observers at the end of the nineteenth century, but descriptions of rural life in the Lower Mississippi Valley acquired a new angle of vision. Travelers from the North and even those from southern cities began to represent traditional subsistence practices as quaint customs, part of a picturesque landscape and a peculiar culture.[54] Although local-color depictions of livelihood in south Louisiana were less derogatory than earlier accounts, these newer writings perpetuated the notion that the region's natural bounty was mainly responsible for a backward way of life. Describing the prairie country between New Iberia and Vermilion Bay for *Harper's Magazine* in 1887, Charles Dudley Warner found between scattered herds of cattle "a cabin here and there, a field of cane or cotton, a garden plot." In Warner's opinion, the inhabitants of Vermilion Parish were a people frozen in time: "Here among the intricate bayous that are their highways and supply them with the poorer sort of fish, and the fair meadows on which their cattle pasture, and where they grow nearly everything their simple habits require, they have for over a century enjoyed a quiet existence, practically undisturbed by the agitations of modern life, ignorant of its progress." Warner stopped at the plantation of Simonette LeBlanc on Bayou Tigre, where the owner and his sons had just returned in a schooner from a fishing and oystering expedition to Vermilion Bay. "Such trips are not uncommon," he reported, "for these people seem to have leisure for enjoyment, and vary the toil of the plantation with the pleasures of fishing and lazy navigation." According to Warner's overall assessment of the Acadian people, they "came into a land and a climate suited to their idiosyncrasies, and which have enabled them to preserve their primitive traits."[55]

Alcée Fortier, a professor of French language and literature at

Tulane University, visited Acadian country in September, 1890, in order to collect material for his study of Louisiana culture and history. Like northern journalists and writers of his own time, as well as earlier generations of officials and observers, this upper-class Creole from New Orleans saw anachronistic folkways being facilitated by natural conditions. "Living is very cheap in the prairie," he observed, "and the small farmers produce on their farms almost everything they use. At the stores they exchange eggs and hens for city goods." He felt that Acadians "form an important and useful part of our population, although many of them are as simple and ignorant as their ancestors in 1755." "They are," Fortier hastened to add, "generally honest and laborious." Traveling to Saint Bernard Parish in June, 1891, Fortier offered a similar account of the Isleños. As was the case in Acadian country, some prominent planter families emerged from this relatively isolated population. "The great majority, however, as with the descendants of the Acadians, are poor and ignorant. They cultivate their little patch of ground and raise vegetables, chiefly potatoes and onions. They are also great hunters."[56] This late-nineteenth-century lens of observation, emphasizing the primitive and picturesque character of creolized agriculture, influenced for a long time the way future students would approach rural life in the Lower Mississippi Valley.

The creolization of agriculture in the Lower Mississippi Valley began in the early eighteenth century when American Indians, European settlers, and African slaves encountered each other in a colonial world. Some of the most enduring forms of intercultural exchange occurred in local subsistence and marketing practices. Methods of farming, in close association with hunting, herding, and other procurement activities, became vital means for sustaining independent households. Creolized subsistence practices allowed a diverse population to maintain some control over its livelihood in face of mounting pressures to participate more fully in a cash-crop economy. The knowledge and resourcefulness discerned by recent scholars as necessary for this adaptation, however, were not recognized by most contemporary observers of the process. Economic strategies pursued by different groups of immigrants over the years were usually criticized by outsiders more interested in rapid commercialization of agriculture. Value judgments attributing greater agency to the environment than to its inhabitants played an important ideological role in the transformation of rural life in the Lower Mississippi Valley, helping conceal the importance of creolization in the region's agricultural history.

Notes

1. Robert A. Hall, Jr., *Pidgin and Creole Languages* (Ithaca: Cornell University Press, 1966); Loreto Todd, *Pidgins and Creoles* (London: Routledge and Kegan Paul, 1974).

2. Edward Brathwaite, *The Development of Creole Society in Jamaica, 1770–1820* (Oxford: Clarendon Press, 1971), p. 296.

3. Joseph G. Tregle, Jr., "Creoles and Americans," in *Creole New Orleans: Race and Americanization*, ed. Arnold R. Hirsch and Joseph Logsdon (Baton Rouge: Louisiana State University Press, 1992), pp. 131–85.

4. For a sample of cookbooks with varying definitions of creole cuisine, see *The Picayune's Creole Cook Book* (1901; reprint, New York: Dover Publications, 1971); Rima Collin and Richard Collin, *The New Orleans Cookbook: Creole, Cajun, and Louisiana French Recipes Past and Present* (New York: Alfred A. Knopf, 1978); and Howard Mitcham, *Creole Gumbo and All That Jazz: A New Orleans Seafood Cookbook* (Reading, Mass.: Addison-Wesley, 1978).

5. James C. Scott, *The Moral Economy of the Peasant: Rebellion and Subsistence in Southeast Asia* (New Haven: Yale University Press, 1976); Stephen Gudeman, *The Demise of a Rural Economy: From Subsistence to Capitalism in a Latin American Village* (London: Routledge and Kegan Paul, 1978); Hebe Maria Mattos de Castro, "Beyond Masters and Slaves: Subsistence Agriculture as a Survival Strategy in Brazil during the Second Half of the Nineteenth Century," in *The Abolition of Slavery and the Aftermath of Emancipation in Brazil*, ed. Rebecca J. Scott (Durham: Duke University Press, 1988); Rhoda Halperin, *The Livelihood of Kin: Making Ends Meet "The Kentucky Way"* (Austin: University of Texas Press, 1990); Stuart Woolf, ed., *Domestic Strategies: Work and Family in France and Italy, 1600–1800* (Cambridge: Cambridge University Press, 1991); Annie Moulin, *Peasantry and Society in France since 1789* (Cambridge: Cambridge University Press, 1991).

6. Steven Hahn and Jonathan Prude, eds., *The Countryside in the Age of Capitalist Transformation: Essays in the Social History of Rural America* (Chapel Hill: University of North Carolina Press, 1985); Christopher Clark, *The Roots of Rural Capitalism: Western Massachusetts, 1780–1860* (Ithaca: Cornell University Press, 1990); Allan Kulikoff, *The Agrarian Origins of American Capitalism* (Charlottesville: University Press of Virginia, 1992).

7. Peter H. Wood, *Black Majority: Negroes in Colonial South Carolina from 1670 through the Stono Rebellion* (New York: Alfred A. Knopf, 1974); Darrett B. Rutman and Anita H. Rutman, *A Place in Time: Middlesex County, Virginia, 1650–1750* (New York: W. W. Norton, 1984); Betty Wood, *Women's Work, Men's Work: The Informal Slave Economies of Lowcountry Georgia* (Athens: University of Georgia Press, 1995); Philip D. Morgan, *Slave Counterpoint: Black Culture in the Eighteenth-Century Chesapeake and Lowcountry* (Chapel Hill: University of North Carolina Press, 1998).

8. Archives des Colonies, Paris, ser. C13A, vol. 44, fol. 58, cited hereafter as AC,C13A, with volume and folio numbers.

9. Daniel H. Usner, Jr., "A Cycle of Lowland Forest Efficiency: The Late Archaic-Woodland Economy of the Lower Mississippi Valley," *Journal of Anthropological Research* 39 (winter, 1983): 433–44.

10. Antoine Le Page du Pratz, *The History of Louisiana*, ed. Joseph G. Tregle, Jr. (London, 1774; facs. repr., Baton Rouge: Louisiana State University Press, 1975), p. 184.

11. Gregory A. Waselkov, "Changing Strategies of Indian Field Location in the Early Historic Southeast," in *People, Plants, and Landscapes: Studies in Paleoethnobotany*, ed. Kristen J. Gremillion (Tuscaloosa: University of Alabama Press, 1997), pp. 179–94. For a general discussion of slash-and-burn agriculture, see Ester Boserup, *The Conditions of Agricultural Growth: The Economics of Agrarian Change under Population Pressure* (Chicago: Aldine, 1965), pp. 15–30; and Marshall D. Sahlins, *Tribesmen* (Englewood Cliffs, N.J.: Prentice-Hall, 1968), pp. 30–31.

12. For the wider context of these production activities, see Gwendolyn Midlo Hall, *Africans in Colonial Louisiana: The Development of Afro-Creole Culture in the Eighteenth Century* (Baton Rouge: Louisiana State University Press, 1992); Daniel H. Usner, Jr., *Indians, Settlers, and Slaves in a Frontier Exchange Economy: The Lower Mississippi Valley before 1783* (Chapel Hill: University of North Carolina Press, 1992); and Thomas N. Ingersoll, *Mammon and Manon in Early New Orleans: The First Slave Society in the Deep South, 1718–1819* (Knoxville: University of Tennessee Press, 1999).

13. Quote is from Reuben Gold Thwaites, ed., *The Jesuit Relations and Allied Documents: Travels and Explorations of the Jesuit Missionaries in New France, 1610–1791*, vol. 67 (Cleveland: Burrows Brothers, 1896–1901), p. 283.

14. Lewis Cecil Gray, *History of Agriculture in the Southern United States to 1860*, vol. 1 (Washington, D.C.: Carnegie Institution, 1933), pp. 337–40; John G. Clark, *New Orleans, 1718–1812: An Economic History* (Baton Rouge: Louisiana State University Press, 1969), pp. 52, 183–86. To compare land distribution in Louisiana with that in Canada, see Richard Colebrook Harris, *The Seigneurial System in Early Canada: A Geographical Study* (Madison: University of Wisconsin Press, 1966), pp. 20–40, 117–38.

15. Heloise H. Cruzat, trans., "Louisiana in 1724: Banet's Report to the Company of the Indies, Dated Paris, December 20, 1724," *Louisiana Historical Quarterly* 12 (Jan., 1929): 121–33; Heloise H. Cruzat, trans., "Sidelights on Louisiana History," *Louisiana Historical Quarterly* 1 (Jan., 1918): 99–100; Thwaites, *Jesuit Relations*, 67:297. Also see Marcel Giraud, *Histoire de la Louisiane française: La Louisiane après le système de Law (1721–1723)* (Paris: Presses Universitaires de France, 1974), pp. 196–215.

16. Le Page du Pratz, *History of Louisiana*, pp. 20–22, 27–28; Jean François Benjamin Dumont de Montigny, "Historical Memoirs of M. Dumont" (1753), in *Historical Collections of Louisiana*, vol. 5, ed. B. F. French (New York: Lamport, Blakeman and Law, 1846–53), p. 31; Charles R. Maduell, Jr., comp. and trans., *The Census Tables for the French Colony of Louisiana from 1699 through 1732* (Baltimore: Genealogical Publishing Co., 1972), pp. 16–27; Glenn R. Conrad, ed. and trans., *Immigration and War: Louisiana, 1718–1721: From the Memoir of Charles Le Gac* (Lafayette: University of Southwestern Louisiana Press, 1970), pp. 61–62.

17. Jacob M. Price, *France and the Chesapeake: A History of the French Tobacco Trades*, vol. 1 (Ann Arbor: University of Michigan Press, 1973), pp. 302–60.

18. *Mississippi Provincial Archives: French Dominion*, vols. 1–3, ed. Dunbar Rowland and Albert Godfrey Sanders (Jackson: Mississippi Department of Archives and History, 1929–32); vols. 4–5, ed. Rowland and Sanders, rev. and ed. Patricia Kay Galloway (Baton Rouge: Louisiana State University Press, 1984), 1:168–70, 2:586–87, 3:637–38, 4:43 (cited hereafter as *MPAFD*); Clark, *New Orleans*, 61–87.

19. An informative glimpse at how plantation laborers divided their time between producing food and producing export crops is given in the diary of William Dunbar, who owned a plantation near Baton Rouge during the 1770s. See Eron Dunbar Rowland, comp., *Life, Letters, and Papers of William Dunbar* (Jackson: Press of the Mississippi Historical Society, 1930), pp. 23–34.

20. "Records of the Superior Council" were published intermittently in the *Louisiana Historical Quarterly* (cited hereafter as *RSCLHQ*), vols. 1–22 (1918–39); see *RSCLHQ*, 5:466–77. Similar farms were common at the settlements of First and Second German Coasts, Pointe Coupée, and Natchitoches, where in 1766 the average number of slaves ranged from 2.5 to 6 per farm. See Jacqueline K. Voorhies, comp. and trans., *Some Late Eighteenth- Century Louisianians: Census Records of the Colony, 1758–1796* (Lafayette: University of Southwestern Louisiana Press, 1973), pp. 163–214.

21. *RSCLHQ*, 8:602–20.

22. Le Page du Pratz, *History of Louisiana*, p. 387. For an insightful reading of the spatial arrangement of slave gardens in another plantation society, see Lydia Mihelic Pulsipher, "The Landscape and Ideational Roles of Caribbean Slave Gardens," in *The Archaeology of Garden and Field*, ed. Naomi F. Miller and Kathryn L. Gleason (Philadelphia: University of Pennsylvania Press, 1994), pp. 202–21.

23. Dumont de Montigny, "Historical Memoirs," p. 120; AC,C13A, 35:39–52; Records and Deliberations of the New Orleans Cabildo, Jan. 10, 1772, Louisiana Division, New Orleans Public Library. Sidney W. Mintz's *Caribbean Transformations* (Chicago: Aldine, 1974), pp. 192–95, laid important groundwork for exploring unsupervised production of food crops by slaves. For recent scholarship on this and other aspects of the internal economy of slaves, see Ira Berlin and Philip D. Morgan, eds., *The Slaves' Economy: Independent Production by Slaves in the Americas* (London: Frank Cass, 1991); Mary Turner, ed., *From Chattel Slaves to Wage Slaves: The Dynamics of Labour Bargaining in the Americas* (Bloomington: Indiana University Press, 1995); and Wood, *Women's Work, Men's Work*.

24. AC,C13A, 14:138; Relation de la Louisiane [c. 1735], 19 (anonymous manuscript), Edward E. Ayer Collection, Newberry Library, Chicago; *MPAFD*, 5:30.

25. T. Jefferys, *The Natural and Civil History of the French Dominions in North and South America* (London: Printed for T. Jefferys, 1761), p. 147; Helmut Blume, *Die Entwicklung der Kulturlandschaft des Mississippideltas in kolonialer Zeit* (Kiel: Im Selbstverlag des Geographisahen Instituts der Universität Kiel, 1956), pp. 50–56; Reinhart Kondert, *The Germans of Colonial Louisiana 1720–1803* (Stuttgart: Hans-Dieter Heinz, 1990), pp. 47–49, 66–71.

26. Charles César Robin, *Voyage to Louisiana, 1803–1805*, trans. Stuart O. Landry, Jr. (New Orleans: Pelican Press, 1966), pp. 114–15; Thomas Ashe, *Travels in America, Performed in 1806* (London: William Sawyer & Co., 1808), pp. 326–27.

27. Voorhies, *Some Late Eighteenth-Century Louisianians*, pp. 181, 263–70, 441–43; Albert J. Robichaux, trans. and ed., *Colonial Settlers along Bayou Lafourche: Louisiana Census Records, 1770–1798* (Harvey, La.: Privately printed, 1974), pp. 9–19.

28. Margaret Jones Bolsterli, "The Very Food We Eat: A Speculation on the Nature of Southern Culture," *Southern Humanities Review* 16 (spring, 1982): 119–27. For the use of maize in the slave trade and the forms of maize consumption in West Africa, see Marvin P. Miracle, *Maize in Tropical Africa* (Madison: University of Wisconsin Press, 1966), pp. 87–106.

29. Elizabeth Donnan, ed., *Documents Illustrative of the History of the Slave Trade to America*, vol. 4 (Washington, D.C.: Carnegie Institution, 1930–35), pp. 635–38; *MPAFD*, 2:310, 351, 3:519–20.

30. Ernest Gueymard, "Louisiana's Creole-Acadian Cuisine," *Revue de Louisiane/Louisiana Review* 2 (summer, 1973): 8–19; John Miller, "A Brief Look at Creole," *Mississippi Folklore Register* 13 (spring, 1979): 33–37; C. Paige Gutierez, "Louisiana Traditional Foodways," in *Louisiana Folklife: A Guide to the State*, ed. Nicholas R. Spitzer (Baton Rouge: Louisiana Folklife Program, 1985), pp. 151–59. For a summary of the etymology of "gumbo," see William A. Read, *Louisiana-French* (Baton Rouge: Louisiana State University Press, 1931), p. 122.

31. R. E. Chandler, "Ulloa and the Acadians," *Louisiana History* 21 (winter, 1980): 90–91.

32. Gilbert C. Din, "Early Spanish Colonization Efforts in Louisiana," *Louisiana Studies* 11 (spring, 1972): 31–49; Gilbert C. Din, "Spanish Immigration to a French Land," *Revue de Louisiane/Louisiana Review* 5 (summer, 1976): 63–80; Robin F. A. Fabel, *The Economy of British West Florida, 1763–1783* (Tuscaloosa: University of Alabama Press, 1988), pp. 6–21.

33. Roger W. Shugg, *Origins of Class Struggle in Louisiana: A Social History of White Farmers and Laborers during Slavery and after, 1840–1875* (Baton Rouge: Louisiana State University Press, 1939), pp. 44–45, 76–79, 94–107; James H. Dorman, *The People Called Cajuns: An Introduction to an Ethnohistory* (Lafayette: University of Southeastern Louisiana Press, 1983), pp. 25–30; Carl A. Brasseaux, *Acadian to Cajun: Transformation of a People, 1803–1877* (Jackson: University Press of Mississippi, 1992), pp. 10–19. This social geography was common in black-belt areas across the South. See Stephanie McCurry, *Masters of Small Worlds: Yeoman Households, Gender Relations, and the Political Culture of the Antebellum South Carolina Low Country* (New York: Oxford University Press, 1995), pp. 22–30.

34. Bernard Romans, *A Concise Natural History of East and West Florida*, facs. reprod. of 1775 ed. (Gainesville: University of Florida Press, 1962), p. 121.

35. Amos Stoddard, *Sketches, Historical and Descriptive, of Louisiana* (Philadelphia: Mathew Carey, 1812), p. 310.

36. Robin, *Voyage to Louisiana*, pp. 114–15.

37. Seargent Prentiss, *Memoir of S. S. Prentiss*, vol. 1, ed. G. L. Prentiss (New York: Charles Scribner, 1855), p. 95.

38. Brasseaux, *Acadian to Cajun*, pp. 10–22; Lauren C. Post, *Cajun Sketches: From the Prairies of Southwest Louisiana* (Baton Rouge: Louisiana State University Press, 1962), pp. 25–31, 70–77; Malcolm L. Comeaux, *Atchafalaya Swamp Life: Settlement and Folk Occupation* (Baton Rouge: Louisiana State University School of Geoscience, 1972), pp. 7–15; J. Paul Leslie, "Laurel Valley Planta-

tion, 1831–1926," in *The Lafourche Country: The People and the Land*, ed. Philip D. Uzee (Lafayette: Center for Louisiana Studies, 1985), pp. 206–208.

39. Ashe, *Travels in America*, pp. 322–31; Gilbert C. Din, *The Canary Islanders of Louisiana* (Baton Rouge: Louisiana State University Press, 1988), pp. 84–104, 124–43.

40. Timothy Flint, *Recollections of the Last Ten Years in the Valley of the Mississippi* (1826), ed. George R. Brooks (Carbondale: Southern Illinois University Press, 1968), pp. 236–37.

41. Joseph Holt Ingraham, *The Southwest. By a Yankee*, vol. 2 (New York: Harper and Brothers, 1835), p. 26.

42. Caroline Bell to Edward George Washington Butler, Mar. 18, 1823, Butler Family Papers 1778–1975, Historic New Orleans Collection, New Orleans, Louisiana.

43. Solomon Northrup, *Twelve Years a Slave*, ed. Sue Eakin and Joseph Logsdon (Baton Rouge: Louisiana State University Press, 1968), pp. 152–55.

44. William Howard Russell, *My Diary North and South*, vol. 1 (London: Bradbury and Evans, 1863), pp. 396, 399. A discerning analysis of slaves' internal economy in the sugar parishes of Louisiana can be found in Roderick A. McDonald, *The Economy and Material Culture of Slaves: Goods and Chattels on the Sugar Plantations of Jamaica and Louisiana* (Baton Rouge: Louisiana State University Press, 1993), pp. 50–91. For an overview of similar production and exchange activities among Mississippi slaves, see Daniel H. Usner, Jr., "Frontier Exchange and Cotton Production: The Slave Economy in Mississippi, 1798–1836," *Slavery and Abolition* 20 (Apr., 1999): 24–37.

45. Frederick Law Olmsted, *The Cotton Kingdom: A Traveller's Observations on Cotton and Slavery in the American Slave States*, ed. Arthur M. Schlesinger (New York: Knopf, 1953), pp. 257–58.

46. Russell, *My Diary North and South*, pp. 403–404.

47. The complexity of this relationship is brilliantly captured in the novels of Ernest J. Gaines, especially *Catherine Carmier* (1964), *Of Love and Dust* (1967), and *A Gathering of Old Men* (1983).

48. Shugg, *Origins of Class Struggle in Louisiana*, pp. 94–111, 262–73; Donald Holley, *Uncle Sam's Farmers: The New Deal Communities in the Lower Mississippi Valley* (Urbana: University of Illinois Press, 1975), pp. 3–14; Albert E. Cowdrey, *This Land, This South: An Environmental History* (Lexington: University of Kentucky Press, 1987), pp. 107–24; John M. Barry, *Rising Tide: The Great Mississippi Flood of 1927 and How It Changed America* (New York: Simon and Schuster, 1997).

49. Tony Dunbar, *Our Land Too* (New York: Pantheon, 1971), pp. 26–27.

50. William H. Harris, ed., *Louisiana Products, Resources and Attractions, with a Sketch of the Parishes: A Hand Book of Reliable Information Concerning the State* (New Orleans: E. A. Brandao and Co., 1881), p. 105.

51. Post, *Cajun Sketches*, p. 74.

52. Frank M. Lovrich, *The Social System of a Rural Yugoslav-American Community: Oysterville* (San Francisco: R and E Research Associates, 1971), pp. 111–20; John V. Baiamonte, Jr., *Immigrants in Rural America: A Study of the Italians of Tangipahoa Parish, Louisiana* (New York: Garland, 1990), pp. 64–96.

53. Joseph V. Guillotte III, "Creolization and Ethnicity," in *Louisiana Folklife: A*

Guide to the State, ed. Nicholas R. Spitzer (Baton Rouge: Louisiana Folklife Program, 1985), pp. 65–73; Christopher A. Airriess and David L. Clawson, "Vietnamese Market Gardens in New Orleans," *Geographical Review* 84 (Jan., 1994): 16–31.

54. For an insightful analysis of this literature, see Nina Silber, *The Romance of Reunion: Northerners and the South, 1865–1900* (Chapel Hill: University of North Carolina Press, 1993), pp. 66–92.

55. Charles Dudley Warner, *Studies in the South and West with Comments on Canada,* in *The Complete Writings of Charles Dudley Warner,* vol. 8, ed. Thomas R. Lounsbury (Hartford, Conn.: American Publishing Co., 1904), pp. 86–110.

56. Alcée Fortier, *Louisiana Studies. Literature, Customs and Dialects, History and Education* (New Orleans: F. F. Hansell and Bro., 1894), pp. 163, 179–80, 199–200.

Decoctions for Carolinians

Mary L. Galvin

The Creation of a Creole Medicine Chest in Colonial South Carolina

Lethal diseases, illness, and natural hazards such as rattlesnakes posed a challenge to colonial settlement and survival in the semitropical regions of the Americas. In South Carolina the colonizers (including Europeans and the involuntary African immigrants) faced serious health hazards related to their new physical and social environment. To assure their survival and population growth, the newcomers had to adopt measures for dealing with a variety of unhealthful conditions.[1] In colonial South Carolina, Europeans and Africans addressed the health hazards of their new environment by seeking new knowledge from the indigenous population and from each other, by attempting to apply their existing knowledge to new situations, and through experimentation.

Sidney Mintz and Richard Price have constructed a basic framework for creolization studies that is applicable to colonial South Carolina. First, cultural transfers should be treated as one element of analysis, but as no group can "transfer its way of life and the accompanying beliefs and values intact from one locale to another," close attention must also be paid to the changes the experience generated.[2] By examining the migrants' responses to the health hazards posed by their relocation, we can further our understanding of the factors influencing the process of cultural borrowing and cultural evolution as well as cultural transfer.

Second, we must attempt to identify the grammatical and lexical components of both the heritage and the new hybrid cultures.[3] The lexical component of healing would include the medicines and tools used to heal a patient. The grammatical component is the group's causal explanation for illness, its understanding of how the body functions, and the method of treatment. This essay will focus on an essential element in the lexical component of healing: the creation of a Carolinian medicine chest. However, to analyze the relative importance of borrowing and transfer in any aspect of the development of a creole culture, we must keep the beliefs and practices of the heritage cultures in full view in order to identify variation or change in the hybrid culture. Therefore, a brief discussion of this aspect of healing is included here.[4]

Finally, in European colonies reliant on enslaved African labor the imbalance of power and status affected cultural evolution, but it did not necessarily favor European cultural transfer in all cases.[5] Political, social, and economic power are not the only determinants of cultural selection. Carolinian healing practices were clearly influenced by the environment, the interaction of cultural groups, the enslaved status of Africans, and the minority status of Europeans.

Although they recognize the deep divisions separating Africans and Europeans in the colonial setting, Mintz and Price suggest that "the interpenetration of these sectors poses one of the most interesting and enigmatic questions to be weighed in examining the growth and character of so-called creole societies."[6] Because the peoples who lived in colonial South Carolina were sharply divided by status and access to power, Carolinian culture includes the subcultures created by both Africans and Europeans. These subcultures can be analyzed separately, but they did not function as separate entities in the manner of neighboring societies. Rather, it was through their interaction that Carolinian culture evolved. The creole Carolinian culture and subcultures were also influenced by the indigenous peoples in their midst and on their frontier. South Carolina is surely a good place to begin addressing questions of cultural interaction.

Creolization is a process of selective adaption in which borrowing is affected but by no means determined by the newcomers' sense of self-importance relative to the indigenous population. The ideology of English colonization incorporated a strong sense of British cultural superiority, which English settlers and visitors frequently displayed.[7] Yet only the most stubborn people would scorn the knowledge and skills of people they regarded as inferior if these subordinate people could provide cures and preventatives in an alien environment.

For European settlers, borrowing played an essential role in the development of creole healing practices in colonial South

Carolina. One of the earliest surviving English accounts testifying to the desire to acquire Indian medical knowledge is contained in a 1680 letter written by Maurice Mathews:

> I am little skilled in the phisicall nature of vegetables but I have by my interest with some charge upon the Indians gained a knowledge of severall of their secrets in the use of roots barks leaves and Some trees, I have seen admirable cures by simples and spare dyet in a short time performed by Indians in veneriall and Scurbitick distempers I have also known speedy assistance given unto women in labor I mean Inglish & Indian women by our Nighbor Indians, by giving them decocted in water certane roots.[8]

Mathews claimed to have collected medical recipes and requested that someone with knowledge of physic be sent to analyze what he had learned, but unfortunately he did not include the recipes in this surviving correspondence.

The account of John Lawson provides an example of the tension created when specific needs confronted the Eurocarolinians' ideology of cultural superiority in the selective borrowing process. While noting that Indian efforts at curing themselves of foreign diseases, especially smallpox, were ineffectual, Lawson admitted that:

> you may find among 'em Practitioners that have extraordinary Skill and Success in removing those morbifick Qualities which afflict 'em, not often going above 100 Yards from their Abode for their Remedies.... An Indian hath been often found to heal an English-man of a Malady, for the Value of a Match-Coat; which the ablest of our English Pretenders in America, after repeated Applications, have deserted the Patient as incurable; God having Furnish'd every Country with specifick Remedies for their Peculiar Diseases.[9]

Despite the barb aimed at Eurocarolinian practitioners, Lawson was not implying that Indians were culturally superior or more knowledgeable than Europeans in general. He carefully preceded and followed this acknowledgment of indigenous skills with qualifiers, stating that whereas Indian remedies were useless against smallpox and other European diseases, he did believe that Indians had the knowledge requisite to control a number of local health problems. Lawson considered it important that the colonizers access this "God-given" knowledge.

The British naturalist Mark Catesby, who visited South Carolina in 1722, was less impressed by indigenous healing skills than were most colonists. He attributed the Indians' "happy constitution of body" to "their little use of physic, and their superficial knowledge therein." After a brief description of a few Indian practices Catesby declared, "*Indians* are wholly ignorant in Anatomy, and their Knowledge in Surgery very superficial; Amputation and Phlebotomy they are strangers to; *yet they know many vulnerary and other Plants of virtue, which they apply with good Success. . . ."*[10]

While these examples illustrate the varied attitudes toward borrowing on the part of European colonizers, Mintz and Price note that diasporan Africans displayed "a general openness to ideas and usages from other cultural traditions."[11] Although Afrocarolinians were also selective in creating a new culture and individual responses to borrowing surely varied, their status in the colony had a greater impact on what was available to them from the material cultures of their heritage complex. They could create much from memory, but their ability to import plants, seeds, or drugs of their choice was severely limited. Moreover, the heterogeneity of the enslaved community provided numerous African traditions from which selections could be made in addition to those borrowed from Indians and Europeans.

Unfortunately we do not have firsthand written accounts to document the responses of Africans to indigenous healing practices. However, because Eurocarolinians were active Indian slave traders, the enslaved population included a significant proportion of Amerindians in the early decades of colonization—25 percent in 1708—when borrowing was an essential strategy employed by Africans.[12] We also know that Africans and Indians lived in close and apparently harmonious contact.[13] Marriages between these groups occurred in autonomous Indian communities and between free and enslaved people, as well as within the enslaved population on the plantations, indicating that there were no social taboos preventing intermarriage.

Certain commonalities enhanced the likelihood that close contact between Africans and Indians in the enslaved community would favor the incorporation of Indian knowledge in creole healing practices. Most important, the semitropical environment of South Carolina produced a disease environment and botanical and faunal types that were somewhat familiar to Africans. From the brief descriptions below it is also apparent that African and Amerindian views on illness and healing practices shared much in common prior to their contact and cohabitation.

To understand what was borrowed, transferred, and invented in the process of creolization in Carolinian healing ways, we must first briefly examine the beliefs and practices associated with healing for each group. "Eurocarolinian," "Afrocarolinian," and "Amerindian" are all terms for population categories containing peoples from diverse cultural heritages. Any analysis of the transfer of one group's practices is based on attributes found in its heritage groups. At the level of a particular ritual or practice there is much variation within these larger categories. However, common threads also ran through the beliefs and practices of each of these regionally defined heritage groups that provide a basis for differentiating among them.[14] Additionally, there are areas where two or all three of the groups had certain practices or beliefs in common. We must not draw the lines between these heritage groups too sharply. All were functioning in a "prescientific" world and practiced homeopathic medicine with varied results.

Eurocarolinian physicians based their healing practices on the teachings of Galen, a Greek physician whose treatises had informed European medical practice since the second century. Galen's humoral theory stated that the body contained four fluids—blood, phlegm, choler (yellow bile), and melancholy (black bile)—which must be kept in balance and untainted to maintain good health and temperament. Morbid humors were treated with botanical medicines—to promote urination (diuretic), induce sweating (diaphoretic), induce vomiting (emetic), and open the bowels (purge)—and/or with bleeding (phlebotomy) or blistering to let off blood, thereby depleting the body of excess or contaminated fluids and restoring balance to the system.

Europeans also generally accepted the concept that the climate or "air" played an important role in negatively or positively influencing the balance of the humors. In the eighteenth century they debated new theories involving chemical, mechanical, and pathological explanations for illness. This led to an increasing emphasis on observation, but treatment was little affected by the debate, and "humoral doctrine continued to be held by many practitioners throughout the eighteenth [century] and into the nineteenth century."[15] The main impact of the shift to empiricism may have been the addition of new drugs to the pharmacopoeia. Because of greatly increased contact with new botanical specimens, this expansion of pharmacological knowledge was well suited to, and partially fueled by, the colonial experience. Colonization also heightened the attention paid to climatic conditions as both the climate and health problems varied greatly from colony to colony.

In colonial South Carolina the division of expertise maintained in European medical practice was blurred. A colonial physician was called upon to treat all types of illness and act as an apothecary, yet most healers were not medical doctors.[16] Thomas Dale, a graduate of Leyden who settled in Charleston in 1725, provides us with a good example of the former. In a letter to a friend in London he described himself as "Dr, Apothe, Surgeon, Man-midwife, Druggist & Chymist, besides Judge & Justice of the peace."[17] However, domestic medicine (health care administered by family members) and reliance upon neighbors or practitioners with a local reputation for healing were more common than resort to a medical doctor.[18] Furthermore, Eurocarolinians sometimes employed supernatural explanations of causation in tandem with or in place of anatomical and environmental ones. For some, perhaps even the majority, acts of God or the malevolence of humans acting on their own or the devil's behalf continued to hold explanatory power for misfortune, including illness, in the eighteenth century.[19]

In western and central African societies medicine was deeply affected by religion, which was a key component of all community social activity. Healers were priests and priestesses in these cultures where illness and injury (like all misfortune) were believed to have supernatural causation.[20] Misfortune could befall one as a result of one's own antisocial behavior that might cause offended ancestors to intervene. Ancestors or deities might act of their own accord for unknown reasons. Witchcraft, the malevolent act of a human preying upon others, could also be the cause of misfortune. In general, there is an underlying concept of human or spirit action that results in illness as a response to social imbalance.

Africans carried their ritual authority and healing practices throughout the diaspora, where they took various forms. In the

United States these healers were known largely as "conjurors" and "root-persons."[21] Historic African healing practices have been summarized by John Mbiti:

> The medicine man is in effect both doctor and pastor to the sick person. His medicines are made from plants, herbs, powders, bones, seeds, roots, juices, leaves, liquids, minerals, charcoal and the like; and in dealing with a patient, he may apply massages, needles or thorns, and he may bleed the patient, he may jump over the patient, he may use incantations and ventriloquism, and he may ask the patient to perform various things like sacrificing a chick or goat, observing some taboos or avoiding certain foods, and persons—all these are in addition to giving the patient physical medicines.[22]

In all societies determining the source of an illness is essential to the cure. For Africans, diagnosis included discovering the metaphysical cause of the physical symptoms. If the patient's behavior was at fault, that patient would need to make amends to placate the ancestor or deity responsible; if witchcraft was the cause, the witch's power must be reversed by the healer. As Mbiti points out, the application of medicines could only be effective when the patient and healer addressed the supernatural cause of the illness.

Botanical roots played an important role in African and Afrocarolinian healing as both the source of medications and as charms. Robert Farris Thompson tells us that "according to Kongo mythology, the very first *nkisi* given to man by God was Funza, distributor of all *minkisi* [plural], himself incarnate in unusual twisted-root formations." Africans and African Americans considered twisted roots very powerful as charms to heal an existing condition and to protect one from illness or other misfortune. Roots also contain power as the source of drugs which were used for healing and poisoning by Afrocarolinians.[23]

Southeastern Indian beliefs about the cause of illness reflected their belief in a balanced connection between humans, animals, and plants as interrelated elements in the cosmos. "So long as men behaved properly and remained pure," wrote Charles Hudson, "and so long as they did not cause the forces in nature to become unbalanced, things went well in human affairs." Illness, injury, or death had two possible explanations. Primarily, illness followed when humans killed animals without attaining their consent. Animals responded by inflicting illness. Humans then had recourse to plants to cure themselves. The Cherokee legend that delineates this relationship directs humans to experiment with the pharmacological properties of plants to determine how they could be effectively used for healing.[24]

Indian healing required the abilities to discern the cause of illness (which could require divination), to select the proper plants, and to prepare and administer them to effect. Expertise in healing was one of the skills held and passed on by religious leaders. Treatment was twofold: manipulation, dietary restrictions, scarification, and herbal medicines were employed to treat the specific symptoms, and the appropriate rituals were performed to restore balance in the cosmos. "For the Cherokees, and probably other Southeastern Indians," avers Charles Hudson, "the main strategy in a curing ceremony was to cure the illness by invoking the spiritual enemies of whatever was causing the illness."[25]

Indians also recognized witchcraft as a cause of illness or death. Conjury was a common practice, "which any normal person might resort to . . . to attain his ends, but witchcraft was peculiar to witches, who were not human beings at all, but were heartless monsters who only appeared to be human." A priest held the power to cause misfortune and illness and to counter the conjuring of others. But "an intrinsically vague and uncertain distinction existed between a priest who used conjuring to cause a man to fall ill, go mad, or die and a witch who could do the same." According to Hudson, priests used conjuring in socially acceptable ways, but witches caused illness and death to rob the victim of life years, which were added to their own. Priests used countermagic against witches to reestablish purity, and discovered witches were summarily executed.[26]

All of the culture groups interacting in colonial South Carolina shared a focus on the concept of imbalance in their beliefs regarding causation, and they all relied heavily on botanical (and to a lesser extent faunal) medicines in their healing practices. Despite some intra- and intergroup divergence in their specific causal explanations, their practices often converged in treating an illness. Treatment for many medical problems such as snakebite and cuts and bruises from an injury might be less reliant on balancing the humors or the cosmos than would treatment for those illnesses with less obvious sources.[27] But even in those cases where differing beliefs in causation were paramount to the healer, an equally essential part of the treatment could be interchangeable among these belief systems because it was based on botanical medicines and perceived results.

"Fevers," parasitical worms, venereal disease, and rattlesnakes were prominent among the health hazards that threatened the lives and vigor of the newcomers to South Carolina. By isolating specific problems in this manner, we can attempt to determine the factors influencing particular responses. An examination of the methods adopted for treatment in these cases illustrates some important avenues of lexical change—borrowing, adaptation of prior knowledge, and discovery through experimentation—in the creolization process.

One eighteenth-century medical tract listed "Intermittents of all kinds" among the acute diseases most frequent in Charleston and its neighborhood.[28] Peter Wood has noted that these "fevers," particularly malaria and yellow fever, constituted "the greatest health hazard confronted by Europeans settling in the subtropical southern Atlantic regions."[29] Commonly called the "Ague," malaria found a local vector in the mosquitoes that abounded on the rice and indigo plantations of the low country. Malaria was not indigenous to the Americas, and the mild form present in the European population, vivax, was not a grave health danger.[30] However, once Africans came in large numbers to any region with suitable conditions for the vector, the more virulent strain common in Africa, falciparum, became a major health problem. The deadly yellow fever, another mosquito-borne disease, was also endemic along the coast of West Africa and uncommon, but not unknown, in Europe.

Afrocarolinians suffered less from both strains of malaria due to genetic factors. A significant percentage of the West African and African American population are immune to vivax malaria because they lack Duffy-positive red blood cells. Afrocarolinians who carried the sickle cell trait (probably 30 percent) had milder cases and a reduced mortality rate from falciparum malaria. Afrocarolinians also benefited from the acquired immunity of antibodies they carried with them from West Africa, where the disease was endemic. Mothers passed the antibodies on to their infants during pregnancy. Similar antibodies were present in the West African population for the less prevalent, but more deadly, yellow fever. Because Eurocarolinians had no genetic immunities either to falciparum malaria or to yellow fever, and because the development of acquired immunities requires several generations to become relatively effective, they experienced the more severe and chronic cases of malaria and higher mortality rates from both malaria and yellow fever.

Europeans' adaptation to new ecosystems in the Americas varied greatly according to region. In New England life expectancy increased, while it decreased markedly in the Chesapeake, South Carolina, and the Caribbean.[31] The slave societies of North America were infamous for the high mortality rate among newcomers known as "seasoning." In the Lowcountry, this was a prominent feature of colonization throughout the eighteenth century. However, as settlement grew, so did the occurrence and virulence of lethal and debilitating diseases. Because of the particular environment, commercial crops pursued, and mixture of people and pathogens, all Carolinians confronted escalating health hazards. Caught in this spiral, Eurocarolinians sought to transplant, import, and discover local medicinal plants to cool their temperatures, purge their bodies, and restore balance to their humors.

The physical environment often played a decisive role in the selection process for medicinal (and other) plants. Although the European colonists had sufficient access to the seeds and plants of their heritage cultures, the plants commonly found in English physic gardens did not always fare well in the soils and climate of Carolina. Monk's rhubarb, a species of dock used as a purgative, provides a good example of ecological determination. The early English colonists evidently attempted to grow monk's, for Lawson saw it in physic gardens during his travels.[32] In 1713 Pryce Hughes penned a proposal to the duchess of Ormond requesting funding for a colony of poor Welsh to be settled in the Carolina interior, near the Cherokee. He also wrote an accompanying letter of instructions to a Brother Jones in which he stated that he had "begun a History of ye plants of ye country" and designed "to make a Physick garden," requesting the seeds of plants that "do not grow here, as Rhubarb," among others.[33] In 1724 Catesby composed a list of physic plants he "would like to introduce" into Carolina; he wondered "whether Rhubarb if it could be procured would agree with their Clymate."[34] At midcentury Dr. Alexander Garden, a prominent Charleston physician and avid naturalist, maintained one of the best physic gardens in colonial South Carolina. Through careful cultivation and to his surprise, Garden was able to get a second-year growth of rhubarb from seeds sent him by an English correspondent.[35] Despite these efforts to introduce English and perhaps other varieties of dock and rhubarb, Governor Drayton did not list any species of rhubarb among the "exotics" domesticated in South Carolina at the end of the century.[36]

Another import, Peruvian bark, was elevated to preferred status in the treatment of intermittent fevers by the eighteenth century. This bark, of the South American cinchona tree, may well have been effective in relieving malarial symptoms or their recurrence as the cinchonas are a source of medicinal quinine. But there is no evidence that it was cultivated in South Carolina. Despite one observer's comment that Carolinians commonly chewed the bark, access would have been limited to those who could procure imported drugs.[37] Like rhubarb, Peruvian bark was expensive and not always readily available for purchase.

Indigenous plants were commonly employed to treat "fever" symptoms, and their use as substitutes for rhubarb or Peruvian bark was noted in contemporary documents. For example, Carolinians frequently relied on the bark of the southeastern tulip tree as a local substitute for Peruvian bark. In his catalog of indigenous plants and their uses, Gov. John Drayton noted that "in intermittents, [the tulip tree] is supposed by many to be little inferior to Peruvian bark."[38] In addition to the tulip tree, two other indigenous plants stand out as common local substitutes. Indian physic or Bowman's root was considered an "efficacious emetic" and was believed "to possess a tonic power . . . thought peculiarly beneficial in the intermittent fever."[39] One scholar of American medicinal botany states, "the emetic property of this root was well known to the Aborigines."[40] Indian physic was classified as *Euphorbia Ipecacuanhae*, or American ipecac, although it does not belong to the cinchona family. The common and scientific names given to this plant clearly indicate both its association with Indians and its medicinal use by Europeans. This colonial association of an indigenous plant with the medical qualities of the cinchonas also applies to the may apple *(Podophyllum)*, which according to Catesby was also called "Ipecacuana" in South Carolina.[41] May apple was "one of the principal remedies used by the American aborigines, by whom it is especially valued on account of its cathartic action."[42] Carolinians also employed other local fever medicaments such as the Virginia snakeroot, dogwood, and "thorough-wort, which was used by Indians as medicine in intermittent fevers."[43]

Intestinal worms posed another constant and serious health hazard to colonists.[44] They infested people of all ages, classes, and ethnicities. According to Dr. Milligen-Johnston, "worm fevers are very frequent, and common to all ages, though children under five years of age suffer most, particularly in the Spring and the beginning of Summer." The increased problem in the spring and summer seasons can be at least partially explained by two factors. First, Milligen-Johnston noted, "the Sweet Potato, Indian Common Maize, and Pompion, all much used in the diet seem to have a larger share of the eggs of the mischievous Insects, than the rest of the farinaceous or leguminous kind," and these crops were grown, ripened, and eaten at this time of the year.[45] Milligen-Johnston's association of these plants with the eggs of intestinal worms is puzzling, as the life cycle of the parasite and means of contraction were not known to him, and he was probably observing plant-eating worms. However, if these plants were fertilized with human feces or exposed to contaminated water, or if defecation in or near the fields and gardens was common, roundworm eggs could have been transmitted via the plants or the dirt that accompanied them to the house. Second, and more important, there is probably a link between the season and children as the primary hosts. Small children, who usually played outside in the warm months clad only in shirtlike garments, would have been running around barefoot and frequently sitting bare-bottomed in the dirt. Given the unsanitary conditions of the era, they would have picked up numerous eggs that could have entered either through their skin and orifices or orally via dirty hands. To treat intestinal worms, Milligen-Johnston wrote, "I know of no medicine more likely to be of Service then the Decoction of Pink-root."[46]

According to all sources, colonial newcomers learned early of the Indian treatment for this condition. The Cherokee called the plant *Unsteetla,* while the colonists referred to it as Indian pink or pinkroot.[47] Parasitical worms are known the world over, and peoples have discovered various vermifugal plants in their environs to destroy and purge them from the body.[48] It is safe to assume that some of these parasites had been a health problem for the indigenous population. As people universally seek solutions to such problems, it seems most likely that the Cherokee, or some other group living in the region where pinkroot grew, had discovered its powerful vermifugal qualities. Due to the effectiveness of this remedy, the plant became a trade item between the indigenous peoples of the coast and the mountains and found its way into the Carolinian pharmacopoeia early in the colonial period. Because of pinkroot's particular growing conditions, production was apparently limited to the interior region controlled by the Cherokee, who remained the source of this important drug throughout the eighteenth century.

Eurocarolinian doctors used the root and published accounts extolling its virtues. Alexander Garden experimented with dosages and prescribed this indigenous treatment regularly. In bills to his friend and patient Richard Bohun Baker he listed charges for worm purges, and the regular correspondence between Garden and Baker frequently refers to the cases of worms and worm fever that especially plagued Baker's children.[49] Garden began acquainting his British colleagues with the vermifugal shortly after his arrival in South Carolina in 1752. Between 1753 and 1757 he prepared an informative article entitled "Description, History, and Account of our Pink Root" at the request of Dr. Whytt, his former professor at Edinburgh.[50] The results of his experiments and observations contained in three letters written in 1757, 1764, and 1766 were published in 1771.[51]

The prominence of worm diseases in the Afrocarolinian community is equally attested to in medical and plantation records.[52] An 1804 letter of an overseer, John Cunningham, tells us a great deal about the diagnosis and treatment of two children who probably died from worm fever. Concerning the children's treatment, Cunningham wrote that when they were "taken with a fever last week, Minder Gave them Life Everlasting which took the fever off." Then shifting his focus to possible explanations for the children's deaths, he attempted to exculpate himself in the matter by writing, "it is said by all the Negroes that Nothing was the cause of this death but constant eating of poison Burys [berries]." He blamed Silvay, the mother, because "She did not take her Children to Bed with her." At the end of his narrative he stated, "they had discharged a heap of worms before their deaths and Both have died in one minutes time."[53] Although Cunningham apparently missed or avoided the significance of the worms, the enslaved woman Minder, who treated them, did not. Life everlasting was another plant in the Indian pharmacopoeia that possesses antihelminthic properties.[54] It is not known if Indian pink was available in this case, but it would appear that the healer, Minder, properly diagnosed the problem and applied the best worm remedy at her disposal.

The vermifugals pinkroot and life everlasting provide us with another good example of the importance of indigenous knowledge that was readily borrowed and applied. Eurocarolinians quickly adopted pinkroot and, finding the drug effective, introduced it into the British pharmacopoeia. In his official accounting of the goods exported from Charleston from November, 1750, to November, 1751, Gov. James Glen listed "Indian Pink Root—2 hhds & 5 casks—at—£80."[55] At the end of the century another Carolinian governor declared, "it is an article of great trade with the Cherokee Indians and is sent in Hogs Heads from the neighborhood of the Occonnee Mountain to Charleston for exportation."[56] It is hard to tell how long it might have taken the colonists—unassisted by Amerindians—to find this plant and recognize its antihelminthic qualities. Minder knew that life everlasting was also a vermifugal; like their European counterparts, Africans were equally, if not more, aware of the various plants employed in Indian healing to destroy worms.

The diseases associated with a large pox—yaws, syphilis, and gonorrhea—were also prevalent in colonial South Carolina.[57] As did the diseases associated with fevers and worms, they required treatments that brought together African, Indian, and European knowledge. John Lawson's account illustrates the early association of venereal disease with the Americas. He stated, "We being well enough assured that the Pox had its first rise (known to us) in this New World, it being caught of the Indian Women by the Spanish Soldiers that follow'd Columbus. . . ." He also related a story about an Indian doctor who

> had the misfortune to lose his Nose by the Pox, which Disease the *Indians* often get by the *English* Traders that use amongst them; not but the Natives of *America* have for many Ages (by their own Confession) been afflicted with a Distemper much like the *Lues Venerea* [syphilis], which hath all the symptoms of the Pox, being different in this only; for I could never learn that Country-Distemper, or Yawes, is begun or

continu'd with a Gonorrhoea; yet it is attended with nocturnal Pains in the Limbs, and commonly makes such a Progress as to vent Part of the Matter by Botches, and several Ulcers in the body; and other Parts; oftentimes Death ensuing. I have known mercurial Ungents and Remedies work a Cure, following the same Methods as in the Pox; several white People, but chiefly *Criolos*, losing their Palates and Noses by this devouring Vulture.[58]

Here we have a good example of how problematic the identification of disease and its region of origin could become in this pluralistic environment. The debate among scholars regarding the origins of venereal disease is partly associated with the confusion of observers such as Lawson.[59]

Yaws is not a venereal disease but is caused by a pathogenic bacteria related to that of syphilis and displays similar symptoms. Yaws was carried to the Americas by Africans throughout the era of the slave trade and is transmitted through contact with open sores. Open ulcers and deformation of the bones, nose, and palate characterize the disease. Syphilis also produces a "pox" (ulcerous skin eruptions) and bone lesions, but the hard, red venereal lesions associated with syphilis distinguish it from yaws. It is unknown if Lawson is referring to these lesions as "Gonorrhoea" or if he is also associating gonorrhea with syphilis. It would appear that venereal diseases and yaws were spread back and forth between as well as within culture groups. Without a clear description of the symptoms, however, it is difficult to determine in individual cases which disease is being treated, as all three were referred to as "the Pox," "Yawes," and "venereal disease" in colonial documents. The "venereal disease" cures discussed below were definitely syphilis treatments, but they may also have been used to treat persons suffering from yaws or gonorrhea.

Whatever the source, Europeans suffered from and actively sought cures for venereal disease. Lawson informed his readers that Indians had cures for "the Pox." The "no-nosed" doctor referred to above withdrew to the woods where he perfected a cure "by proper Vegitables & c. of which they have Plenty, and are well acquainted with their specifick Virtue." Of Carolina's Indians in general he stated, "they cure the Pox, by a berry that salivates, as *Mercury* does; yet they use sweating and Decoctions very much with it; as they do, almost on every Occasion; and when they are thoroughly heated they leap into the River."[60] Although Lawson does not identify either the berry or the plants used in decoctions, Drayton and Charles Millspaugh indicate that two indigenous plants, blue Virginian cardinal flower and yaw weed, are noteworthy for their use in decoctions for treating venereal disease.[61]

Blue Virginian cardinal flower is clearly documented as a "borrowed" indigenous treatment for venereal disease. According to Millspaugh, "the natives of North America are said to have held this plant a secret in the cure for syphilis." Sir William Johnson purchased this "secret" and introduced the drug derived from the plant to Europe as a syphilis cure, but it failed to achieve success there. Nonetheless, Linnaeus believed in its efficacy and named the plant *Lobelia syphilitica*. Millspaugh suggests that the European doctors failed to get positive results because they did not use the drug in combination with may-apple *(Podophyllum peltatum)* roots and wild cherry *(Prunus Virginica)* and New Jersey tea *(Ceanothus americanus)* bark as the Indians did. Drayton claimed that New Jersey tea was "excellent for the venerial desease," and Blue Virginian cardinal flower was "used by the Indians for curing the Venerial desease."[62]

Stillingia sylvatica was also considered "excellent for the cure of the Venerial disorder."[63] It was commonly known in Carolina as "Yaw weed" or "Cock-up Hat"—obvious references to its medical application. At the end of the nineteenth century Millspaugh's entry for the plant stated: "For many years before its introduction in medicine . . . as an alterative in syphilis, it had been used in the South, by the laity, as an emetic, cathartic, and alterative; indeed it was and is still considered, in Southern States, an absolute specific in syphilis, entirely superseding the use of mercury."[64] "Entirely superseding" is an exaggeration here, for mercury was still used by some in treating syphilis, but yaw root was in widespread use when the fresh root was available.[65]

Yaws, syphilis, and gonorrhea were health problems in the Carolinian slave community that were treated by both Eurocarolinian and Afrocarolinian doctors. Bills from Dr. Matthew Hardy contain hefty charges of twenty-five pounds each for "curing Prince of the Yaws" and "curing Pheby of a Canker yaw."[66] The Ball family papers include an account book kept by John Ball that records several entries of monies due to and held for Robin, a freedman in his employ as a driver. One entry reads: "I am to pay Robin 30/ for curing Hagar of the venereal disease."[67] We know that treatments for the various "large poxes" developed by Europeans, Africans, and Amerindians were all employed in South Carolina, but more specific information, such as which remedies were employed by Dr. Hardy and Robin, is not available for further analysis.[68]

As did lethal and debilitating diseases, Carolina's reptiles endangered settlement. The colony's promotional literature insisted that early encounters with the rattlesnake did not cause an alarming number of deaths. Nevertheless, this creature's deadly potential and the occasional examples of fatal bites frightened both prospective and actual settlers. The language of the promotional literature alerts us to the widespread perception of danger linked to the rattlesnake. In a letter written to encourage his French émigré friends to join him in Carolina, Louis Thibou wrote in 1683: "As for the rattlesnake, of which there has been much talk in England, you can easily kill it for it does not move more than a tuft of grass; a child could kill one with a switch. It is true that a few people have been bitten by accident, but there is a good remedy for that here and no one has ever died of their bite; all that has been said about this kind of animal is just a lot of fairy-tales."[69] Although Thibou does not identify the "good remedy," he does imply with the word "here" that local knowledge included the necessary curatives.

In his attempt to alleviate the fears of his friends and potential settlers Thibou understated the danger. If encounters with rattlesnakes were of such little consequence, it would be difficult to explain the long and concerted effort to find a cure for its bite. However, the development of commercial agriculture required an enormous effort in land-use renovation. Africans and Europeans cultivated thousands of acres, drained marshes, tapped the forests for lumber and pitch, and cleared building sites. These activities disturbed many snakes, justifying the search for an effective cure.

While most Eurocarolinian accounts note that the rattlesnake was not aggressive and would likely avoid confrontations with humans when possible, the problem was still characterized as formidable, for the snake could turn up anywhere and kill instantaneously. Mark Catesby wrote of several close encounters with rattlesnakes on the footpath at Colonel Blake's house. Once a snake was even discovered in his bed by a servant turning down the bedclothes. Catesby characterized the rattlesnake as the "most deadly venomous Serpent of any in these parts of *America*."[70] Declaring he had "seen and kill'd abundance," John Lawson wrote, the "Bite is venomous, if not speedily remedied; especially if the Wound be in a Vein, Nerve, Tendon, or Sinew; when it is very difficult to cure."[71]

In the colony's early years most Europeans considered Indian expertise regarding rattlesnakes to be the most reliable. The Indians used certain plants as preventatives: "Col. *Moore*, a Gentleman of good Reputation in Carolina, told me [Catesby] that he has seen an Indian daub himself with the Juice of this Plant [purple bind weed of Carolina]; immediately after which, he handled a Rattle-Snake with his naked Hands without receiving any harm from it. . . . And I have heard several others affirm, that they have seen the Indians use a plant to guard themselves against the venom of this sort of snake."[72] Indigenous expertise was also called upon to remedy the bites. Lawson echoed other early accounts when he observed: "the *Indians* are the best Physicians for the bite of these and all other venomous Creatures of this country. There are four sorts of Snake Roots already discovered which knowledge came from the *Indians* who have performed several great cures."[73]

Catesby was more skeptical regarding remedies. He did not have much faith in the roots that the Indians "pretend will effect the cure. These the *Indians* carry dry in their Pockets" to "chew, and swallow the Juice, applying some to the Wound."[74] He noted that their practice of sucking the wound was a successful remedy if the bite was slight. However, "Where a Rattle-Snake with full Force penetrates with his deadly Fangs, and pricks a Vein or Artery, inevitable Death ensues."[75] Catesby then added, "I could heartily wish, that Oil of Olives immediately applied to the Wound, might have as good Success against the Venom of these Snakes, as it hath been found in *England* to have had against the Poison of the common Adder."[76]

While Lawson and other colonists clearly demonstrated a reliance on indigenous expertise, Catesby illustrates another common response pattern to an observed or learned problem in the colonial setting. First, he examined the solution applied by those more familiar than himself with the problem. In this case he found their solution only partially acceptable—sucking worked if the bite was slight. Then he searched his own knowledge for a comparable case and proposed the olive oil. In this, as in many cases, prior knowledge did not provide a viable solution. Despite his skepticism, Catesby wrote to the Royal Society that he hoped to send them "Specimens of all the kinds of Snakeroots some of which are not known in Virginia."[77]

It would also appear that any new claim to a cure was given a hearing. In one well-advertised example there was an attempt to introduce a foreign cure in the early 1740s. Imported "Chinese Snake-Stones" were purported to "effectually cure the Bites of all venomous and poisonous Creatures as rattle (and other) Snakes, Scorpions, mad Dogs, & small cancers." It was claimed that the stone, applied to the wound, would draw out and absorb the venom. The stones were supposedly practical, as they would "purge" themselves of the absorbed poisons upon immersion in water and could be reused "an Hundred times."[78] Although it created a temporary stir, this cure does not appear to have been widely used or accepted.

No evidence could be found that European colonists or Eurocarolinians discovered a snakebite remedy through experimentation with snakeroots or any other local plants.[79] Afrocarolinians, however, were more actively collecting and cultivating snakeroots and devising medical compounds to remedy the bite. Regarding the Virginia snakeroot, Catesby stated, "the Negro Slaves (who only dig it) employ much of the little time allowed them by the Masters in search of it."[80] There were a number of incentives for them to do so. For one, cash could be earned by gathering or cultivating the roots for sale. For example, a Charleston doctor, Samuel Carne, advertised that he would give five shillings per pound "for any quantity of SNAKE-ROOT, and if clear'd from the leaf, 7 s 6."[81]

In addition, Africans were largely reliant on indigenous plants for medications and charms. True, some African medicinal plants were grown in the colony, and some medicinal ingredients were included in the provisions on slave ships and could have been disposed of in Charleston. For example, Malegueta pepper, which was carried on most slave ships, "was used to prepare both food and beverages and was thought to prevent dysentery and stomach disorders, the major scourges of the middle passage."[82] Also, some plants imported from Europe and other places were available, but these were not easily accessible and did not sufficiently fill the need. Thus, it was incumbent upon Afrocarolinians to learn as much as they could, as quickly as possible, to adapt their healing practices to their new surroundings.

Health care in the slave community was commonly administered by enslaved healers. While many slave owners called in Eurocarolinian doctors to treat sick Africans, this practice was curbed by the limited availability and considerable expense of these practitioners.[83] As discussed above, African healing required spiritual knowledge that Eurocarolinian doctors and planters neither possessed nor sought, and this healing style provided psychological benefits to the patient. Therefore, it is highly likely that enslaved people preferred black doctors. In the cases of snakebite wounds, which usually require early treatment for a high recovery rate, Afrocarolinian healers would have been most readily at hand when slaves were in need of treatment. Constituting the majority of the population and the rural workforce, Africans probably encountered rattlesnakes frequently enough that discovering a remedy became a high priority for Afrocarolinian doctors.

Because they needed effective treatments but had limited access to the medicines of their heritage cultures, enslaved African healers proved to be the most creative cultural innovators on the scene. "Doctor Caesar of South Carolina in St. Paul's Parish, Practitioner of Physick," developed a snakebite remedy calling for doses of root juice from wild horehound and plantain.[84] The wound was treated with a good tobacco leaf moistened with rum. Plantain *(Plantago)* is found in many parts of the world, but it is believed that the plant was introduced into the Southeast by Europeans.[85] Scots applied the leaves to wounds and sores, and the seeds were used for coughs. However, this Afrocarolinian recipe calls for use of the root, from which a decoction was made, rather than use of the leaf as a vulnerary. Further, various contemporary references to a "wild" plantain could indicate that an indigenous plant with properties similar to plantain was being used. Tobacco is, of course, associated with numerous ritualistic and medicinal uses among Amerindians, including using the leaf as a vulnerary. In his *History of the American Indians,* James Adair stated that, to his knowledge, Indians carried "a piece of the best snake-root, such as the *Seneeka,* or fern-snake root,—or the wild hore-hound, wild plantain, St. Andrew's cross, and a variety of other herbs and roots, which are plenty, and well known to those who range the American woods" as snakebite remedies.[86] In creating his remedies Doctor Caesar must have engaged in much experimentation, seeking out plants whose properties would be similar to those he was familiar with in Africa and/or borrowing from indigenous Americans (or those who had acquired this knowledge from them) to perfect his cure.[87] As the lengthy poison cure clearly indicates, Doctor Caesar could easily communicate a remedy that was not only in the English language but also conformed to European medical sensibilities. Unfortunately, the available records do not indicate whether or not Doctor Caesar used a different method when administering to African patients.

Another example of a snakebite remedy attests to the evolution of creole practices evolving in the Afrocarolinian community just a decade later. Sampson's remedy contained "Heart-Snake" (or Hartsnake) root, which Catesby identified as one of the roots commonly used by Indians for snakebite.[88] Sampson also scarified the wound before applying bruised herbs to it, and he used green herbs whenever possible. The main ingredient (and perhaps others as well) and some elements of the application, such as scarifying the wound, are consistent with southeastern Indian medical practices. It is likely that Sampson was also using a creole remedy that was largely influenced by Indian knowledge and practice.

Enslaved healers such as Doctor Caesar and Sampson were usually familiar with poisons and their antidotes. Eurocarolinians deemed this knowledge necessary to their survival in the volatile social environment created by enslavement, as well as when they were confronted with the bite of a poisonous snake. The importance placed on snakebite cures in the eighteenth century may be inseparable from the use of poisoning as a tool of resistance to enslavement. In Doctor Caesar's case, a clear link is discernible, as the recipes for both poison cures are similar, and the two recipes were usually published together (see appendix).

The evidence indicates that members of the legislature considered these cures the personal intellectual property of the inventor or practitioner. On November 24, 1749, a member informed the House that Doctor Caesar had cured several inhabitants "who had been poisoned by Slaves" and "was willing to make a Discovery of the Remedy which he makes Use of in such Cases for a reasonable reward." A committee was appointed to "consider of and report what Reward the said Negro Man Caesar shall merit for his services." In exchange for his poison and snakebite cures, Doctor Caesar demanded "his Freedom and a moderate Competence [of one hundred pounds per annum] for Life."[89] In Sampson's case, a motion was made and the legislature appointed a committee "to consider and report to the House the most effectual way to procure a discovery of [his] Cure for the Bite of Rattle Snakes." This committee recommended that Sampson "be freed at public expence and have some allowance to support him during his natural life."[90] In both cases the committees determined the efficacy of the cures on the basis of the healer's reputation. In addition to his more general and highly reputed practice treating Afrocarolinians, Caesar had cured a number of prominent slave owners who believed they had been poisoned; and Sampson's ability to cure snakebite poisoning was widely known.[91] Both men personally appeared before the legislature and publicly accepted the terms prior to divulging their secret remedies.

As the above examples show, Eurocarolinians were perfectly willing to tap the knowledge and genius of the people they considered their social and cultural inferiors. In the cases of Sampson and Doctor Caesar, the acknowledgment of white Carolinians was a public matter and the healers were held in high esteem. Hartsnake root "is still commonly known in the South as Sampson's snakeroot."[92] According to Gov. John Drayton, *Gentiana Virginia* was called "Sampson's snake-root" in South Carolina, after Sampson.[93] As it was common practice for Europeans to name plants after distinguished naturalists and medical doctors, and the latter plant was not one of the ingredients in Sampson's remedy, the use of his name here may be an acknowledgment of his contribution to Carolinian medicine. The cures purchased by the legislature were published in the *South Carolina Gazette* and a number of almanacs, making the remedies widely available to the public.

It is also likely that a number of Afrocarolinian cures were passed on to planters in a much less dramatic way than were the rattlesnake remedies of Doctor Caesar and Sampson. According to Alexander Garden's biographers, "It was very apparent that the Africans' knowledge of plants was superior to that of South Carolina doctors," for Garden wrote of them, "if it were not for what they learn from the Negro Strollers and Old Women, I doubt that they would know a Common Dock [rhubarb] from a

Cabbage Stock."⁹⁴ Garden, as the most eminent British-trained doctor in the colony, clearly considered himself above the average practitioner in South Carolina, black or white, but his comment further illustrates that Afrocarolinian medical knowledge crossed racial and class boundaries.

Some Afrocarolinians had regular access to Eurocarolinian doctors. The records of several planters indicate that they sought such services, often at the behest of the ill person. When Davy, a carpenter at Ralph Izard's Round Savanna plantation, was taken ill, the overseer employed a physician immediately, and Alice Izard instructed that "every attention might be paid to him."⁹⁵ Similarly, when Beck informed Mrs. Izard that her daughter Juba had great difficulty swallowing, a doctor of high repute was called, and a delicate surgery was performed to remove a growth. In letters to her husband Margaret Manigault included several references to the complaints of and medical attention given to Joe, William, and Guy.⁹⁶ In these and several other cases the patients involved were artisans or workers who had close contact with a wealthy planter family. Thus, they could request such medical attention when they desired it.

Although field workers were most commonly treated by family members and African healers, medical services were also provided by the planters (male and female) and by Eurocarolinian doctors. Richard Bohun Baker's accounts indicate that doctors fairly frequently visited his plantation to treat black patients for wounds, sores, and illnesses such as pleurisy, yaws, worms, and smallpox. These Afrocarolinians were bled, blistered, sweated, vomited, and purged just as their Eurocarolinian counterparts were.⁹⁷ Although highly debated among Eurocarolinians, the African practice of inoculation was used to prevent smallpox. The African origin of this preventative practice was documented by Cotton Mather. It is not known if Afrocarolinians also used this method in their own communities, but planter documents clearly illustrate that they were inoculated along with Eurocarolinians, and this treatment appears to have been administered on a voluntary basis.

As has been discussed, Carolinians transferred, borrowed, and invented healing practices as they created a creole pharmacopoeia and more varied methods of treatment. The European colonizers of South Carolina measured success in the wealth they were able to create through the production of export crops and exploitation of enslaved producers. Africans were faced with the problem of adapting to a new environment under the constraints of their oppressed status. The main factors influencing the cultural selection process under these economic and social imperatives were the ecosystem, the interaction of culture groups, demography, and the distribution of power.

The ecosystem functioned to influence healing ways primarily through the relationships of humans to plants, animals, and pathogens. In the cases of malaria and yellow fever, the mosquito multiplied rapidly as its habitat was improved through the construction of rice fields and indigo dams. As mosquitoes fed on human blood, they spread the imported pathogens throughout the human population. The danger associated with the bite of the rattlesnake also increased proportionately as the environment was altered for settlement and commercial production. Parasitical worms thrived in the highly productive gardens and under the unsanitary conditions of colonial South Carolina. Yaws and venereal diseases were spread throughout the population through physical human contact. In response to the health hazards they encountered, Carolinians sought out plants with medicinal properties to heal them and relieve their symptoms.

Plants were identified through experimentation and by tapping the knowledge of the indigenous population. Although indigenous Americans were unable to use their medical knowledge to resist the pathogenic onslaught of foreign diseases, they clearly contributed much to the pharmacopoeia and health of the creoles who took their place. Contact between the indigenous peoples and newcomers took various forms, but in the early years of settlement its frequent and often intimate nature provided a conduit for cultural borrowing.

Africans and Europeans also exchanged medical knowledge and used each other's cures on a selective but regular basis. The social relations of slavery in South Carolina were highly influenced by the demographic imbalance. This factor influenced numerous aspects of the culture, including the evolution of a system that relied on trade-offs and client-patron relationships in addition to the use of terror and police force to maintain Eurocarolinian power. In the cases of Doctor Caesar, Sampson, and Robin planters valued the knowledge of the people they held in bondage, but they did not have unlimited power to exploit African expertise and creativity. Thus, creolization in the lexical component of healing was strongly affected by the environment and cultural interaction. The extent of this interaction in both subcultures can be measured by identifying the several ingredients found in a basic creole medicine chest used by the majority of Carolinians.

APPENDIX

Afrocarolinian Poison and Snakebite Cures

Caesar's Cure for Poison

Take the Roots of Plantane and wild Hoare-hound, fresh or dried, three Ounces; boil them together in two Quarts of Water to one Quart, and strain it; of this Decoction let the Patient take one third Part three Mornings fasting successively, from which if he finds any Relief, it must be continued till he is perfectly recovered. On the Contrary, if he finds no Alteration after the third Dose, it is a Sign that the Patient has either not been poisoned at all, or that it has been with such Poison as Caesar's Antidotes will not remedy, so may leave off the Decoction. During the Cure the Patient must live on a spare Diet, and abstain from eating Mutton, Pork, Butter, or any other fat or oily Food.

N.B. The Plantane or Hoar Hound will, either of them, cure alone, but they are most efficacious together.

In Summer you may take one Handful of the Roots and Branches of each, in Place of the three Ounces of the Roots of each.

For Drink during the Cure, let them take the following,

Take the Roots of Golden Rod, six Ounces, or in Summer two large Handfuls of the Roots and Branches together, and boil them in two Quarts of Water to one Quart (to which may be added a little Hoare Hound and Sassafras); to this Decoction, after it is strained, add a Glass of Rum or Brandy, and sweeten it with Sugar for ordinary Drink.

Sometimes an inward Fever attends such as are poisoned for which he orders the following,

Take a Pint of Wood Ashes and three Pints of Water; stir and mix them well together; let them stand all Night, and strain or decant the Lye of[f] in the Morning, of which ten

Ounces may be taken six Mornings following, warmed or cold, according to the Weather. These medicines have no sensible Operation, though sometimes they work in the Bowels, and give a gentle Stool.

The Symtoms attending such as are poisoned are as follows,

A Pain of the Breast, Difficulty of breathing, a Load at the Pit of the Stomach, an irregular Pulse, burning and violent Pains of the Viscera above and below the Navel, very restless at Night, sometimes wandering Pains over the whole Body, a Reaching and Inclination to vomit, profuse Sweats (which prove always serviceable), slimy Stools both when costive and loose, the Face of a pale and yellow Colour, sometimes a Pain and Inflamation of the Throat; the Appetite is generally weak, and some cannot eat any; those who have been long poisoned are generally very feeble and weak in their Limbs, sometimes spit a great Deal; the whole Skin peals, and likewise the Hair falls off.

Caesar's Cure for the Bite of a Rattlesnake

Take of the Roots of Plantane or Hoare Hound, (in Summer Roots and Branches together) a sufficient Quantity, bruise them in a Mortar, and squeeze out the Juice, of which give, as soon as possible, one large Spoonful; if he is swelled you must force it down his Throat. This generally will cure, but, if the Patient finds no Relief in an Hour after, you may give another spoonful, which never fails.

If the Roots are dried, they must be moistened with a little Water.

To the wound may be applied, a Leaf of good Tobacco moistened with Rum.[98]

Sampson's Cure

Dr. Caw acquainted the House that a Committee was appointed by the late Assembly to examine the Negro Sampson, who was manumitted by the Public, concerning his Cure for the bites of Snakes. . . . And that they had examined the said Negro Sampson accordingly. . . .

The Cure for the bites of a Rattle Snake by Sampson, a Negro.

Take Heart Snake Root, both Root and Leaves, two Handfuls, Polypody leaves one handful, bruise them in a Mortar, press out a Spoonful of the Juice and give as soon as possible after the bite, then scarify the wound, and take the Root of the Herb Avens, bruise it, po(u)r a little Rum over it, and apply to the part, over which is to be put the Hartsnake Root and Polypody which remains after the Juice is squeez'd out. These Medecines and Applications must be repeated according to the Violence of the Symptoms, so as in some dangerous Cases it must be given to the quantity of eight teaspoonfuls in an Hour and the wound dressed two or three times a day.

The above Herbs may also be bruised and beat up into a Paste with Clay, and when necessary may be scraped down to the Quantity of half a common Spoonful and given amongst a little Rum and Water, and repeated as the Dozes of the Juice above mentioned. A little of this Paste may be wet with Rum and rubbed over the Wound.

N.B. He always uses this method when he can't find the Green Herbs.

Sometimes the cure is entirely performed by the Patients chewing the Hartsnake Root and swallowing the Juice and applying some of the same Herb bruised to the Wound.

When the part is greatly inflamed and swelled, all the Herbs in the following List are taken to the quantity of some Handfuls of each and boiled into a strong decoction with which it is fomented several times a day.

The herbs presented last by Sampson are,

1. Asarum cyclamini, or Hartsnake Root of this Province.
2. Polypodium Vulgare, or Common Polypody.
3. Caryphyllata Virginiana radice inodora, or Virginia avens, called here five fingers.
4. Lonchitis aspera, or Rough Spleenwort.
5. Hypnum julaceum, or small erect Clubmoss.
6. Gnaphalium humile, or Creeping Goldy Locks.[99]

Notes

1. In the Americas these hazards did not include any indigenous diseases with a genocidal mortality rate. This is in contrast to the West African case, in which it has been convincingly argued that the Europeans' inability to survive the malarial environment of the hinterland, prior to the discovery of quinine's impact on the disease in the late nineteenth century, played a major role in prohibiting earlier colonization. See Daniel R. Headrick, *Tools of Empire* (New York: Oxford University Press, 1981).

2. Sidney W. Mintz and Richard Price, *The Birth of African-American Culture: An Anthropological Perspective* (Boston: Beacon Press, 1992), p. 1. This study uses Mintz and Price's framework selectively.
3. Ibid., chap. 1, passim.
4. The dissertation from which this essay is extracted devotes a separate chapter to a fuller discussion and analysis of medical belief systems and their evolution in the colony ("Piecing Together a Colonial Quilt: Creolization in Early South Carolina," dissertation in progress at the University of California, Los Angeles, Department of History, under the direction of Professor Gary B. Nash). The admittedly brief treatment of background information included here is meant to provide readers with a fuller context for the analysis of the medicines used, which is the focus of this essay; regrettably, both aspects of the topic could not be presented in an essay of this length. The reader will also note that there is a much fuller presentation of European ideas regarding body functions, as I am still attempting to gather information on this aspect in African and indigenous cultures.
5. Mintz and Price, *Birth of African-American Culture,* pp. 3–5.
6. Ibid., p. 5.
7. See Nicholas P. Canny, "The Ideology of English Colonization: From Ireland to America," in *Colonial American Essays in Politics and Social Development,* ed. Stanley N. Katz and John M. Murrin (New York: Alfred A. Knopf, 1983), pp. 47–68.
8. Letter from N:Mathews, Charlstowne, May 18, 1680, South Caroliniana Library (hereafter referred to as SCL); for a published version see *South Carolina Historical Magazine* 55 (1954): 153–59.
9. John Lawson journeyed through Carolina in 1701, traded with the Indians, and settled in North Carolina as a surveyor. In 1709 he published a volume entitled *A New Voyage to Carolina,* which contained "a Journal of A Thousand Miles Travel among the Indians, from South to North Carolina," written in 1700/1701; a natural history entitled "A Description of North Carolina"; and "An Account of the Indians of North Carolina." His stated purpose was to acquaint English readers with the region's "Curiosities worthy [of] a nice Observation." (John Lawson, *A New Voyage to Carolina* [London, 1709], ed. Hugh Talmage Lefler [Chapel Hill: University of North Carolina Press, 1967], pp. 5, 17–18.)
10. Mark Catesby, *The Natural History of Carolina, Florida and the Bahama Islands,* vol. 1 (London, 1731), p. xv, italics added.
11. Mintz and Price, *Birth of African-American Culture,* p. 51.
12. Robert Weir, *Colonial South Carolina: A History* (Millwood, N.Y.: KTO Press, 1983), p. 26; J. Leitch Wright, Jr., *The Only Land They Knew: The Tragic Story of the American Indians in the Old South* (New York: The Free Press, 1981), pp. 130–50; for population data see Peter Wood, "The Changing Population of the Colonial South: An Overview by Race and Region, 1685–1790," in *Powhatan's Mantle,* ed. Peter H. Wood, Gregory A. Waselkov, and M. Thomas Hatley (Lincoln: University of Nebraska Press, 1989), p. 47. Mintz and Price argue that local slave cultures developed at a rapid pace and continued to exhibit a dynamic nature in the Caribbean; see Mintz and Price, *Birth of African-American Culture,* chap. 4, passim.
13. Although there are scattered references in Eurocarolinian documents to a perceived "natural animosity" between Africans and Indians, which have

been quoted in the historical literature, examples of the interactive behavior of the two groups generally contradict this characterization. There are numerous cases of persons claiming both Native American and African ancestry in the legal records of the region, particularly during periods when the laws became more restrictive for free blacks and during the forced removal campaigns of the nineteenth century. Runaway slave advertisements in the *South Carolina Gazette (SCG)* also refer to escapees of mixed ethnicity. For a discussion of "Mustees" in the enslaved population, see Peter Wood, *Black Majority: Negroes in Colonial South Carolina from 1670 through the Stono Rebellion* (New York: W. W. Norton, 1974), p. 99.

14. Mintz and Price dismiss the concept that a common "culture" can be identified for regions such as western and central Africa that incorporate numerous culture groups. However, they promote an alternative thesis that a common "heritage" not only existed but also served as the basis for the creation of African American cultures. See Mintz and Price, *Birth of African-American Culture*, chap. 1, passim.

15. Richard Shryock, *Medicine and Society in America 1660–1860* (New York: New York University Press, 1960), p. 51. This study provides the basic outline of Euroamerican medical thought and practice used here. See also John Duffy, *From Humors to Medical Science*, 2d ed. (Urbana: University of Illinois Press, 1993).

16. The terms "physician" and "medical doctor" will be used herein to denote those healers who identified themselves as such in contemporary documents; these were largely, but not exclusively, those with professional medical training in European colleges.

17. Thomas Dale to Rev. Thomas Birch, Oct. 2, 1735, SCL.

18. See Charles Hudson, *The Southeastern Indians* (Knoxville: University of Tennessee Press, 1976), p. 343, in which Hudson states that this was also the case among the Cherokee; it was/is probably a common enough practice to be considered universal.

19. See Richard Godbeer, *The Devil's Dominion* (New York: Cambridge University Press, 1992) on the transfer of European witchcraft beliefs to the American colonies. Surviving documentation overwhelmingly represents the view of British-trained medical doctors and elite Eurocarolinians but clearly is not representative of the full range of medical beliefs and practices operating among Eurocarolinians.

20. Margaret Washington Creel, *"A Peculiar People"; Slave Religion and Community-Culture among the Gullahs* (New York: New York University Press, 1988), p. 56.

21. Robert Farris Thompson, *Flash of the Spirit: African and Afro-American Art and Philosophy* (New York: Vintage Books, Random House, 1984), p. 107. Thompson's study has had an enormous influence on the study of the cultures of diasporan Africans. He identified numerous examples of African, particularly Bakongo, influence in diasporan art and belief systems. In *"Peculiar People"* Margaret Creel has argued that Bakongo influence is strong in the religion of the Gullah of the South Carolina low country.

22. John S. Mbiti, *African Religions and Philosophies* (New York: Heinemann, 1969), p. 165; quoted in Creel, *"Peculiar People,"* p. 56.

23. See Thompson, *Flash of the Spirit*, p. 131. An *nkisi* is a charm used by Bakongo ritual experts in healing. Numerous forms of *minkisi* are found in Af-

rica and throughout the African diaspora. All of the cultural groups, although perhaps not all individuals, residing in South Carolina used charms in their attempts to improve various aspects of life, including their health. The power of twisted roots maintains potency in African and diasporan beliefs. See Wood, *Black Majority,* chap. 11 for an analysis of poisoning by Afro-carolinians.

24. Hudson, *Southeastern Indians,* pp. 336, 156–59.
25. Ibid., p. 346.
26. Ibid., pp. 351, 362.
27. Treatment for wounds will be referred to as "vulnerary."
28. George Milligen-Johnston, *A Short Description of the Province of South-Carolina with an Account of the Air, Weather, and Diseases,* at Charles-Town, Written in the Year 1763 (London: Printed for John Hilton, 1770) in Chapman J. Milling, ed., *Colonial South Carolina: Two Contemporary Descriptions* (Columbia: University of South Carolina Press, 1951), p. 153.
29. Wood, *Black Majority,* p. 80. The information on malaria and yellow fever that follows is from Wood, *Black Majority,* pp. 80–91 and from Todd Savitt, *Medicine and Slavery* (Urbana: University of Illinois Press, 1978), pp. 27–32, 240–46.
30. In St. Julien Ravenel Childs, *Malaria and Colonization in the Carolina Low Country, 1526–1696* (Baltimore, 1940), the author argues that malaria was present in England in the seventeenth century and was carried to the colonies by English settlers. Although Childs notes the shift in the virulence of malaria in the eighteenth century and the concurrent growth of the African segment of the population, he does not make any explicit link between the two facts.
31. While longevity is notable among European migrants and their descendants in New England, the effects of that climate on Africans who suffered from greater mortality due to respiratory illness has not been studied. Of course, the devastation of indigenous populations throughout the hemisphere is now well known.
32. Lawson, *New Voyage,* pp. 83–84.
33. Pryce Hughes to Brother Jones, c. 1713, SCL. Hughes was probably referring to monk's here, but other references to efforts to introduce rhubarb may have been to other varieties that English botanists were experimenting with in their attempts to cultivate a "True Rhubarb," which was highly preferred as a purgative but was imported from China at great expense. Clifford M. Foust, *Rhubarb: The Wondrous Drug* (Princeton, N.J.: Princeton University Press, 1992) provides a comprehensive treatment of the quest by Europeans to cultivate a rhubarb with medicinal properties equivalent to the imported varieties.
34. Jan. 16, 1723/24, "Dr. Sherard's Philosophical Letters," Royal Society Library, SCL. Although this is housed with the Sherard letters, it is written to an unknown correspondent (perhaps Hans Sloane), as Sherard is mentioned in the letter in the third person.
35. Letter from Alexander Garden to John Ellis, May 6, 1757, in H. Roy Merrens, ed., *The Colonial South Carolina Scene: Contemporary Views, 1697–1774* (Columbia: University of South Carolina Press, 1977), p. 211.
36. This list first appeared in John Drayton, *View of South Carolina* (Charleston, S.C.: Printed by W. P. Young, 1802), pp. 84–87.

37. The visitor is quoted in Wood, *Black Majority*, p. 76.
38. John Drayton, *The Carolinian Florist* (1807), pp. 60–61. Drayton's manuscript was made available to a limited audience when he donated it to the University of South Carolina in 1807, but it was not published until 1943. References in this text will be cited with the author's name and manuscript title, but page numbers will refer to the appropriate pages in the more accessible published version: Margaret Babcock Meriwether, ed., *The Carolinian Florist of Governor John Drayton of South Carolina* (Columbia, S.C.: South Carolina Library of the University of South Carolina, 1943), which reproduces the text but necessarily alters the pagination.
39. Ibid., p. 55.
40. Charles F. Millspaugh, *American Medicinal Plants* (New York: Dover Publications, 1974), p. 149.
41. Catesby, *Natural History*, 1:24.
42. Millspaugh, *American Medicinal Plants*, pp. 61–64. See also Catesby, *Natural History*, 1:24; Drayton, *Carolinian Florist*, p. 58.
43. Benjamin S. Barton, *Collections for an Essay toward a Materia Medica of the United States* (Philadelphia, Part First, 2d ed., 1801; Part Second, 1804), Part First, p. 27; quoted in Drayton, *Carolinian Florist*, p. 82.
44. For a thorough discussion regarding parasitical worms in antebellum Virginia, see Savitt, *Medicine and Slavery*, pp. 63–73, which is the source of the technical information presented in this section.
45. Milligen-Johnston, *A Short Description*, p. 67. Pompion is pumpkin, and South Carolina's production of farinaceous grains such as wheat was largely limited to the backcountry.
46. Ibid.
47. *Spigelia Marilandica*. See Millspaugh, *American Medicinal Plants*, p. 131.
48. Drugs that destroy and purge worms are called vermifugals or antihelminthics.
49. Baker-Grimke Papers, South Carolina Historical Society (hereafter, SCHS).
50. Edmund Berkeley and Dorothy Berkeley, *Dr. Alexander Garden of Charles Town* (Chapel Hill: University of North Carolina Press, 1969), pp. 29–31, 22. Doctors John Lining and John Moultrie, Jr., also sent samples of pinkroot to England in the 1750s. The drug was being exported to England at this time, but these men were sending samples to their British counterparts for analysis.
51. Alexander Garden, M. D., "An Account of the Indian Pink," *Essays and Observations, Physical and Literary* 3 (1771): 145–53. An earlier and brief account was published in the same journal by Lining in 1754 (1:386–89).
52. Savitt has identified the tapeworm *(Taenia)* and common roundworm *(Ascaris)* as the most prevalent among the varieties of worms infecting Virginia slave communities. This would appear to be the case in South Carolina as well.
53. John Cunningham to Mrs. Moultrie, Mar. 9, 1804, William Moultrie Papers, SCL. From the tone of the letter Minder appears to be a recognized African healer on this plantation.
54. *Gnaphalium*. See Millspaugh, *American Medicinal Plants*, p. 89.

55. James Glen, "An Accot. Of all the Goods Exported from Charles Town of the Produce of South Carolina, from the 1st Novemr. 1750 inclusive, to the 1st Novemr. 1751 exclusive, & the supposed value thereof, in that period, at Charles Town Market," SCL.
56. Drayton, *Carolinian Florist*, p. 20. Drayton's entry for pinkroot also notes, "it is an excellent Anthelmentic; and as such, is generally used in this State successfully in worm cases."
57. For a more thorough treatment of yaws and venereal disease, see Savitt, *Medicine and Slavery*, pp. 73–80, which serves as the basis for information presented here.
58. Lawson, *New Voyage*, p. 25.
59. See Virgil J. Vogel, *American Indian Medicine* (Norman: University of Oklahoma Press, 1970), pp. 56, 152–53, 210–11 for a discussion of this debate.
60. Lawson, *New Voyage*, pp. 26, 226.
61. Drayton, *Carolinian Florist*, pp. 87, 101; Millspaugh *American Medicinal Plants*, pp. 98, 151.
62. Millspaugh, *American Medicinal Plants*, pp. 382–84; Drayton, *Carolinian Florist*, pp. 24, 87.
63. Drayton, *Carolinian Florist*, p. 101.
64. Millspaugh, *American Medicinal Plants*, p. 151. Other uses are noted as well.
65. T. C. Cox's *Medical Vade Medicum* (Charleston, S.C.: Printed by T. C. Cox, 1800) recommended a mercurial ointment. This booklet apparently accompanied a household medicine kit, so it would not have included remedies using fresh herbs.
66. Bill for medical services, Richard Bohun Baker to Matthew Hardy, Jan., 1763, to May, 1764, Baker Grimke Papers, SCHS.
67. Ball Family Papers, "Account Book 1788–1812," account with Jo. Willingham, 1795, SCHS, 11/515/6.
68. In Virginia an African American healer, James Papan, was granted his freedom and an annuity for divulging his cures that had secured "the preservation of the lives of a great number of Slaves belonging to the Inhabitants of the Country, frequently infected with Yaws, and other venereal distempers"; see *Virginia Council Journals, 1726–1753*, Apr. 29, 1729. Papan's cures were made widely available to Carolinians when the *South Carolina Gazette* published them on Mar. 31, 1733; see Wood, *Black Majority*, p. 289.
69. Letter of Louis Thibou, Sept. 20, 1683, SCL. For another example of this type of letter see Peter Purry, "A Description of the Province of South Carolina . . . 1731," in B. R. Carroll, ed., *Historical Collections of South Carolina* (New York: Harper & Brothers, 1836), pp. 136–37. Purry's proposal to Swiss émigrés also indicates the continued concern with the problem of rattlesnakes.
70. Catesby, *Natural History*, 2:41.
71. Lawson, *New Voyage*, p. 134.
72. Catesby, *Natural History*, 1:35.
73. Lawson, *New Voyage*, p. 134. Most early descriptive accounts of any length mention the rattlesnake and the use of roots by Amerindians as a preventative or cure for the bite.
74. Catesby, *Natural History*, 2:41. Catesby names "Assarum Heart-Snake" and

75. "St. Anthony's Cross" specifically as two roots held in esteem and commonly used, but he refers here to an unnamed "small tuberous root." Ibid. A similar remark was made in a letter to Dr. Sherard dated June 20, 1722, SCL.

76. Ibid.

77. Letter to Dr. Sherard, June 20, 1722, SCL. Snakeroot is a category of root based on appearance. Not all of these were used in snakebite remedies, and most had various medical applications.

78. Francis Torres, 1744 broadside, SCL.

79. In 1720 and 1723 a Captain Hall undertook experiments with two different medical practitioners; they failed to produce a remedy. See Joseph Waring, *A History of Medicine in South Carolina, 1670–1825* (Columbia: South Carolina Medical Association, 1964), p. 32.

80. Catesby, *Natural History*, 1:29.

81. *SCG*, June 18, 1750. Catesby stated the price in the 1720s as "6 pence a Pound when dried, which Money is hardly earned"; see Catesby, *Natural History*, 1:29.

82. Robert L. Hall, "Savoring Africa in the New World," in *Seeds of Change*, ed. Herman J. Viola and Carolyn Margolis (Washington D.C.: Smithsonian Institution Press, 1991), p. 167.

83. Often these doctors were not available to treat patients in the rural areas. In correspondence between Dr. Alexander Garden and Richard Bohun Baker, Garden repeatedly apologizes for not being able to get away from his patients in Charleston to treat Baker's family. See Baker-Grimke Papers, SCHS.

84. This is the title that freedman Dr. Caesar addressed himself by in his will, May 17, 1754, Charleston County Wills, 7, pp. 176–77, South Carolina Department of Archives and History; *SCG*, May 14, 1750. This recipe says *"Plantane or Hoare-hound,"* but Caesar's poison cure that precedes it says that "they are most efficacious together."

85. Millspaugh, *American Medicinal Plants*, pp. 419–22. Millspaugh further advised his readers that "Plantain has also been highly praised as an antidote to the effects of bites of venomous reptiles and insects . . . one of the principal ingredients in the remedy of the Negro Caesar."

86. Samuel Cole Williams, ed., *Adair's History of the American Indians* (Johnson City, Tenn.: Watauga Press, 1930), pp. 247–48.

87. Philip Morgan, *Slave Counterpoint: Black Culture in the Eighteenth-Century Chesapeake & Lowcountry* (Chapel Hill: University of North Carolina Press, 1998), p. 625. Morgan bases the identification of Doctor Caesar as an African on Alexander Garden's notation that "a native African had revealed an antidote for poisons three years earlier" in a letter dated Jan. 21, 1753, p. 617 and ftn. 102, p. 618.

88. Catesby, *Natural History*, 2:41.

89. J. H. Easterby, ed., *The Journal of the Commons House of Assembly: March 28, 1749–March 19, 1750* (Columbia: University of South Carolina Press, 1962), pp. 293, 303.

90. Terry W. Lipscomb, ed., *The Journal of the Commons House of Assembly; November 21, 1752–September 6, 1754* (Columbia: University of South Carolina Press, 1983), pp. 313, 320.

91. For an account of Dr. Caesar's reputation, see testimony made before the House, Nov. 29, 1749, in Easterby, *Journal of the Commons House of Assembly,* p. 303; for Sampson, see the committee's report, Jan. 17, 1754, in Lipscomb, *Journal of the Commons House of Assembly,* p. 320.
92. Lipscomb, *Journal of the Commons House of Assembly,* p. xxviii. Lipscomb also notes that the name was "applied to several unrelated species of plants, including the Catesby gentian" discussed below.
93. Drayton, *Carolinian Florist,* p. 26.
94. Berkeley and Berkeley, *Dr. Alexander Garden,* pp. 31–32.
95. Alice Izard to Ralph Izard, Feb. 16, 1795, SCL.
96. Margaret Manigault to Gabriel Manigault, Dec., 1791, SCHS. He also writes on this topic to her.
97. The Baker-Grimke Papers, SCHS, contain bills from David Oliphant and Alexander Garden, Alexander Garden, Matthew Hardy, and Fothringham and McNeill.
98. Easterby, *Journal of the Commons House of Assembly,* p. 479; also published in the *South Carolina Gazette,* May 14, 1750.
99. Lipscomb, *Journal of the Commons House of Assembly,* pp. 144–45.

Drums and Power

Ways of Creolizing Music

in Coastal South Carolina and Georgia, 1730–90

Richard Cullen Rath

Creolization gave African Americans a way to craft autonomous agendas in colonial America, even during slavery. Autonomous agendas are *not* autonomous lives. For Africans in the Americas, slavery precluded the latter in an obvious way. A focus on how they framed their agendas and approached their lives requires a shift in the questions that historians ask. A good deal of work has been done on resistance *to* slavery. An inquiry into how Americans of African descent negotiated their everyday lives needs to include another question too: *With what* did Africans in the Americas frame their agendas? The traditional answers have been either "with very little" because of the destructive, dehumanizing nature of slavery, or else "with some essential African cultural heritage."

In this essay I propose a synthetic approach to cultural creolization that draws on the link between language and culture. This link is contrasted with syntheses that treat cultural creolization as analogous to, rather than integral to, linguistic creolization. In the second part of the essay I examine how Africans and their descendants in the South Carolina–Georgia low country took advantage of musical creolization in their struggles for self-directed rather than other-directed lives during the eighteenth century.

Creolization, Language, and Culture

How does creolization work? It is a way of forming a "native" identity in a situation where there is no natal society. The process takes place with the *descendants* of forcibly displaced immigrant populations when the immigrants were drawn from more than one source. First-generation immigrants, the ones forcibly displaced, undergo *pidginization,* a more tenuous and provisional process of negotiating linguistic and cultural practices in the face of multiple native identities. Children are often born into these groups in a situation where there is no consensual identity. These children take an unstable polyglot cultural inheritance and create stable creole identities from it. If and when natural increase overtakes forced immigration as the chief means of sustaining the population, then the process of creolization affects the whole society, changing it from a heterogeneous group to a creole society. Creole languages and societies are most often associated with a legacy of slavery, which produced the harsh and disruptive conditions necessary for their formation.[1]

To be useful as a concept, creolization needs to be distinguished from other ways of mixing, creating, and maintaining cultural identities. In addition to distinguishing pidginization from creolization, the demographics of forced labor, mixed origin, displacement, natural increase, racism, and inequality also serve to mark creolization off from other related forms of cultural fashioning such as syncretism, hybridity, transfer, borrowing, retention, or translation. Ignoring the special circumstances of creolization renders it analytically redundant as a term.

Students of cultural creolization have treated it as analogous to linguistic creolization. This analogy is mistaken. Culture is not *like* language; it is integral to language, and language to it. Both are ways in which individuals make sense of their worlds. They are both ways of getting meaning to and from expressible forms. They also make the human landscape comprehensible. Language and culture are two different ways of doing this, each dependent on the other.

The twentieth-century history of the idea of linguistic transformations helps make the relationship between language and cultures explicit. From the 1930s through the 1950s structuralist linguists proposed a sort of rule set, called linguistic transformations, that mapped *culturally specific* underlying grammatical structures onto expressions in a particular language. In 1957 Noam Chomsky argued that these underlying structures of language were in fact universals, part of an innate human capacity for acquiring languages. In Chomsky's "generative" grammar, meaning loaded into these innate structures undergoes a transformation that renders expressions in the speaker's language. At first he and his students emphasized spelling out the transformations, on the premise that they were universal. By the mid-1970s it had become apparent that the ever-increasing stock of transformational rules had become too burdensome and culturally specific to function as an explanation of the human capacity for language. Generativists concluded that the innate parts of human language reside in the underlying structures rather than in the transformations of those structures into actual expressions. Linguistic variation results from differences in the transformations used to produce an expression.[2]

While the underlying structures of human language are to some extent universal and a function of individual minds, the transformations that any language user employs *must* be culturally conditioned to some extent. The alternatives would be either the obviously false proposition that all humans speak and comprehend the same particular language or the untestable conclusion that all humans speak their own private language. Transformations—the *ways* that the meanings packed into universal underlying structures are mapped into particular expressions—are culturally specific.[3]

Such transformations define culture: They are the ways we make sense of our worlds. How they do this will condition, if not determine, how they transform a finite set of underlying structures into infinitely varied yet culturally marked expressions. Culture is not a meaning-loaded underlying structure; nor is it some infinite corpus of expressions. It is the way between them. This idea of culture seems to be a profoundly individualistic or personal definition, and in some ways it is. But the notion of self employed here is relational, making culture the way for individuals to situate themselves in the human landscape. Thus an individual's "culture" will be personalized, perhaps in conflict with the cultures of other members of the same society; it may be geared to dealing with "mixed" societies too. But in order to be culture, it must somehow reckon with the ways of others. Less than that renders it an idiosyncratic and most likely incomprehensible expression, or perhaps art.

This definition of culture as *ways of making sense* has three advantages. First, it places culture in its proper relation to both language and society. Second, variety and conflict no longer have to be explained away, because culture does not exist outside the people constructing it. Third, authenticity and essentialism cease to be issues, because no claims are made about culture as a normative object. This makes it a particularly rewarding definition to apply to models of creolization.

Historians and Creolization

The idea of creole identity has been talked about in three general ways. First, it has been discussed as a general moniker for anyone born in the Americas but with ancestors from elsewhere, including Europe. Jack Greene and Benedict Anderson have each employed this "provincialist" definition of "creole" to explain the emergence of distinctively American identities during the eighteenth century. Anderson, in fact, associates creolization solely with Europeans. Second, it has been used as a historically produced outlook, African in its origins, through which Caribbean authors such as Edward Brathwaite and Edouard Glissant have interpreted the histories of their region. Third, and for the present essay most important, anthropologists and historians have employed linguistic models of creolization to explain the origins of African American culture.[4] One contention of this article is that all of these approaches can be integrated into a powerful explanatory tool by examining how language and culture are related. For that reason my emphasis will be on "linguistic" explanations of cultural creolization.

Historians use linguistic models of creolization as a solution to what is known as the "Herskovits-Frazier debate." At the turn of the twentieth century W. E. B. Du Bois, arguing against a paternalist tradition that denied Africans' having any culture with which to begin, claimed that although slavery damaged African institutions severely, parts persisted—especially in the realms of music and religion—to form the core of African American society. In 1939 the sociologist E. Franklin Frazier mustered evidence that the damage had been much more severe than Du Bois had allowed. American slavery, Frazier contended, had obliterated any usable African past. The anthropologist Melville J. Herskovits countered three years later with a compendium of hundreds of American practices having African precedents.[5]

Frazier's position dominated for several decades in the work of Stanley Elkins, Kenneth Stampp, Daniel Patrick Moynihan, and Eugene Genovese. What Africanisms were to be found, they assumed, were isolated and trivial. The differences between Elkins's and Stampp's views had to do with psychology rather than culture, with Elkins positing a pathological, dysfunctional set of black American personality types and Stampp countering that slave resistance was a well-adapted response to a situation in which one's culture had been stripped away. Moynihan's famous report on the modern effects of slavery's destruction of the black family and Genovese's influential work on slave accommodation and resistance in the totalizing sphere of Hegelian master-slave dialectic also both presume Frazier's version of black American history.⁶

During the 1970s Africanisms grew increasingly difficult to dismiss. In 1972 John Blassingame published *The Slave Community: Plantation Life in the Antebellum South,* which drew extensively from Herskovits's ideas and new research to argue for an autonomous slave community that existed alongside slavery. Herbert Gutman challenged Moynihan's conclusions about black families, using a research approach similar to Blassingame's. It became apparent almost immediately that some middle way between Herskovits's and Frazier's views was needed, for while Blassingame and Gutman had demolished the idea of no African past, it was obvious that the slave trade made the carrying of culture a proposition very different from that undertaken by Europeans.⁷

In 1976, with nods to Du Bois and Brathwaite, the anthropologists Sidney Mintz and Richard Price proposed a structuralist synthesis of Herskovits's and Frazier's positions. Mintz and Price drew an analogy between creolized language and creolized culture that focused inquiry on *culturally specific* "deep structures," in line with older structuralist linguistic theories. Specifically, they compared "underlying values and beliefs" with "unconscious grammatical principles." Mintz and Price contended that values and beliefs, because they existed at a deeper level, had a better chance of surviving the middle passage and planters' culture-stripping strategies than did material objects and surface expressions. Creolized cultures, they contended, were *like* creolized languages, in that African-derived deep structures survived even where the various lexicons and surface expressions might not.⁸

Mintz and Price's essay sparked a generation of groundbreaking studies of African American culture during slavery times that borrowed, extended, and critiqued the notion of cultural creolization using linguistic models. Several of these works returned to creole linguistics to qualify their applications of Mintz and Price's model, using what creolists call the "substratist" approach rather than Mintz and Price's structuralism. Substratists count Herskovits as one of their own, and their approach is similar, mapping Africanisms in the Americas to argue that what is distinctive about creole languages and cultures is to be found in their African features. However, the relationship between creole and regional African identities has proven frustratingly elusive. In most cases Africanisms are either too widely distributed to be considered as distinguishing features or too specific from which to generalize.[9] Two examples serve to illustrate.

First, consider Mintz and Price's scenario of a creolized response to a twin birth, an event that they include, along with insanity, suicide, and other unusual occurrences, in the category of phenomena that "would have required *some* kind of highly specialized ritual attention in almost any West African society in West or Central Africa." The difficulty with this model is that the belief Mintz and Price focus on is so general that it could hardly be considered a distinguishing African feature, amounting to the near-tautology that unusual occurrences are treated as being unusual. The underlying values and beliefs about twin births on which they hinge their analysis are far too widely—perhaps even universally—distributed to be markers of a particular source culture.[10] The fact that twin births are regarded as special in many areas of Africa fails to operate as an explanation, because twin births are regarded as special in many other places too. Most other things that fall under the aegis of "underlying values and beliefs" run into the same problem: The more important they are, the less they can be unambiguously and distinctively assigned to a single "cultural region" (if any such thing can be clearly defined) with any confidence.

Second, consider John Szwed and Robert Farris Thompson's convincing substratist exegesis of the origins of baton twirling. They trace the practice back to northern Kongolese sources, from whence it was transmitted to Haiti. There it took shape in *rara* (large groups of people who parade and dance in the streets), with each participating group led by a fantastically outfitted baton-twirling leader. From there it traveled to New Orleans with many Haitian slaves, spreading thence to Mississippi and finding its way into mainstream U.S. entertainment, namely the football half-time show. Here is a well-documented Africanism, but then the question becomes "So what?" Although Thompson asserts the importance of baton twirling, he never quite gets around to explaining just what it is that is important, or how so.[11]

Thus, at Mintz and Price's underlying level of values and beliefs, we run into universally distributed characteristics where they predicted (in structuralist fashion) culturally specific values and beliefs. But at the substratists' level of concrete expression there is a question of significance: Are persistent Africanisms to be celebrated for their mere survival? The solution to this apparent dilemma involves reconsidering culture not as an analogue to language, but as a related system of representation that both affects and is affected by language. It also involves returning to linguistic theories of creolization.

In the 1980s Derek Bickerton turned the field of creole linguistics on its head by arguing that in the process of creolization, normal channels of transmission were so disrupted (à la Frazier) that the resulting creole came close to being an "unmarked" version of the innate human endowment for language posited by Chomsky. His justification arose from observations about the peculiarities of creole languages. Creolists have long known that creole languages around the world show remarkable similarities in their grammatical constructions. Independent origin theories ("polygenesis") leave too many similarities among far-flung creoles to be explained by chance. Explanations of creole structural similarities that depended on historical contact and diffusion also fell short, because even creole languages that had no possibility of contact with each other have similarities in their grammars. For the past fifteen years Bickerton's "bioprogram hypothesis" has been at the center of research and heated debates in creole linguistics. All but the most resolute substratists now allow that linguistic universals account for at least some of the similarities among creole languages, although the questions of which ones and to what extent are contested, often acridly.[12]

With a single exception, historians have roundly ignored the generative turn in creole linguistics. Two reasons could be proposed. The first is that Bickerton's arguments and his critics' rejoinders turn on technical terms and concepts not in historians' toolboxes. Nor need they be. However, to accept the substratist position as consensus is mistaken, particularly since it cannot explain the widespread similarities observed among creole languages. The second reason is that the idea of an innate structure seems inimical to historical inquiry.[13] This may in fact be so, but it also may be why historical inquiries that are focused on deep structures and underlying values and beliefs have been unable to resolve the Herskovits-Frazier debate.

The tack I take in the rest of this article is to acknowledge the possibility that universal structures may be at work at the "deeper" levels of values and beliefs that Africans carried over with them, instead focusing on the culturally specific *ways* in which creolized descendants of enslaved Africans expressed themselves. I will use eighteenth-century African American music from the Georgia–South Carolina low country as a case study.

Drums and Power

During the 1930s a former slave from Saint Simon's Island, Ben Johnson, recalled from his childhood an old African man, Dembo, who was familiar with the traditional African uses of drums. Dembo used to beat a drum at funerals (and probably at feasts), but his master, the Yale alumnus James Hamilton Couper, banned the practice, ostensibly on religious grounds. Johnson said that Couper did not want drums beaten around the dead. By the 1930s the uses of drums for spiritual and festive occasions had seemingly ceased. But many of the coastal Georgian African Americans remembered the use of drums or someone who knew how to make them, and a few admitted that the practice still exists. While drums may have been scarce, the practice of social representation through complex, culturally specific rhythmic patterns thrived in the work songs and hand-clapping patterns that accompany Sea Island spirituals to this day.[14]

African Americans had solid historical grounds to be reticent about their drums and drumming, reasons that stretched across centuries, continents, ethnicities, and racial divides. For example, the Capuchin missionary Girolamo Merolla described his reaction to drumming in 1682. He lived and worked in Songo, a central African state about 150 miles southeast of Angola that was part of a vast region of closely related societies. He wrote that drums were "commonly made use of at unlawful Feasts and Merry-makings, and [were] beaten upon with the Hands, which nevertheless makes a noise to be heard at a great distance." These drums, he continued, were also used for military signaling, for invoking the other world, and for sending off the dead properly. Merolla claimed that he often went to break up such "Hellish

Practices, But the People always ran away as soon as I ever came up to them, so I could never lay hold on any to make an Example of them."¹⁵ Although Merolla had definite ideas about controlling African practices that he found threatening ("Hellish"), he had only limited agency.

From the beginning of the Atlantic slave trade Europeans knew that drums were powerful tools of state among many West African peoples, but they could not quite comprehend *how* this was so. English planters in the West Indies early associated African drum and horn music with mass uprisings of Africans seeking their freedom. In 1688 Hans Sloane, physician to the governor of Jamaica, observed that slaves on the island "formerly on their Festivals were allowed the use of Trumpets after their Fashion, and Drums. . . . But making use of these in their Wars at home in Africa, it was thought too much inciting them to Rebellion, and so they were prohibited by the Customs of the Island." Barbados followed suit in 1699, banning drums, horns, or "any other loud instruments." Masters were to conduct weekly searches of slave quarters, and any of the named instruments found were to be burned under threat of a fine. In 1711 and again in 1722 Saint Kitts passed laws that banned the slaves "from communicating at a distance by beating drums or blowing horns." In 1717 Jamaica codified its earlier policy forbidding "the gathering of slaves by the beating of drums and blowing of horns."¹⁶

Planters passed laws against drums and drumming several times and in various forms, indicating that their control was less than absolute. European fears were straightforward: They feared drums as loud signals that could lead men on a battlefield. Thus, they banned loud instruments, ignoring quieter ones in their laws. They understood only the ways of military and state drumming that they shared with Africans; planters failed to comprehend how African Americans could represent themselves and their agendas in their music rather than just signal with it.

One particular type of West African court music—that radiating from a Kwa ethnic base centered in the region from eastern Nigeria to modern Ghana—was more than a set of signals. It functioned as an immanent and immediate means of representing and communicating ideas in a repeatable form, somewhat similar to a spoken language. Most Kwa languages are tonal; that is, words can be differentiated on the basis of pitch change. Kwa drummers, able to rely in part on pitch patterns, could produce musical representations akin to a language rather than being a fixed corpus of signals. On the other hand, Mende and western Atlantic languages found to the north of the Kwa regions and central African languages to the south are often tonal but are not "tonemic"—that is, words cannot be distinguished on the basis of pitch, but pitch still forms an aspect of correct pronunciation.[17]

Although North American rice planters knew well the attitudes of Caribbean planters toward African drums and drumming, the instruments were not banned at first in South Carolina. In fact, African slaves were often used as drummers in the militia. Peter Wood suggests that African militia drummers were so prevalent in South Carolina that the job was seen as unattractive by "race conscious Europeans."[18]

The early accommodation to Africans' drumming in South Carolina was uneasy, though. The planters feared the power of western and central African drums and drumming. In 1730, according to a Charleston planter, a group of slaves "conspired to Rise and destroy us" at a dance which featured drumming. The alleged revolt was found out and quelled before the slaves were able to issue a call to arms, however. This drumming was associated with particular Kwa nations but also with their creolized allies. A newspaper article from 1736 reported a foiled uprising in Antigua that involved "Coromantee" (western Kwa) and colony-born factions of slaves. The Coromantee leader announced his intention to stage an uprising "in open Day-light, by a Military Dance and Show, of which the Whites and even the Slaves (who were not Coromantees nor let into the Secret) might be Spectators, and yet ignorant of the Meaning." The "meaning" was delivered by "Drums beating the *Ikem Beat*." This plan was also found out, and many slave executions ensued. Those "let in on the Secret" were enslaved creoles and non-Coromantees. Ethnic identities remained important, but a new, more pan-African culture was taking shape under the creolizing forces of slavery.[19]

Planters paid more attention to ethnicity than to creolization. Rather than banning drums, South Carolina and Georgia rice planters simply did not purchase many Kwa males—though since they were preferred in the wealthier and more established sugar colonies, they were scarcely available in the low country anyway. Mende/western Atlantic and central African slaves were both preferred and available before 1740. Owners constantly sought out about 15 to 20 percent of their slaves from the more northerly Windward Coast of the Mende region, where rice was grown as a staple. Certain ethnicities from this area were thought to be more suitable candidates for skilled trades and household duties as well. For field work, slaves from the Kongo/Angola coastal region and its hinterlands were favored. About 40 percent of all South Carolina slaves were from this region during the years preceding 1740. Many others were bought after being seasoned in the Caribbean.[20]

A notice in a *South Carolina Gazette* from 1733 demonstrates one way that African Americans creolized Kongo/Angolan culture in the Americas under the constraints of slavery. The notice offered a ten-pound reward for the return of Thomas Butler, who had run away from the Vander Dussen plantation upriver from Charleston. Thomas was known in the area as "the *famous* Pushing and Dancing Master." For an owner, especially one as intolerant as Vander Dussen seems to have been, to refer to a slave as "master" seems ironic and unusual.[21] It is doubtful that Butler was the master of any dancing skill of which his owner also partook. Nor is it probable that planters sent their children or slaves to such a master to learn dancing—especially not a style that included "Pushing" as a major feature. Butler, however, was not only a master of "Pushing and Dancing" but was also *"famous"* for it.

Butler's skill was most likely not of his own invention. John Storm Roberts discusses the mid-nineteenth-century popularity enjoyed by a Brazilian form of musical martial art called *capoeira de Angola*, which was practiced by young men, often from central Africa. The art could best be described in two words as pushing and dancing. Capoeira uses musical bows, which are percussive string instruments, to set a tempo that disciplines the movements of two dancers who combat each other in a highly ritualized and graceful manner. The musical bow is a much quieter instrument than a drum and can be quickly made from a flexible green tree limb, a length of string or cord, a small stone, a gourd, and a striking stick.[22] The sound is more percussive than melodic. Perhaps the roots of this pushing and dancing martial art lay in trying to keep traditional combat skills honed with no weapons available and drums proscribed. Such intensely purposeful dancing, performed by a master, would surely attract the attention of planters, but they would not necessarily have comprehended what the dance was representing.

Angolan and Kongolese warriors in Africa also had a form of "Pushing and Dancing." Hand-to-hand combat was still a viable military skill in the early eighteenth century, though it was finally being superannuated by firearms—for which, noted the feared warrior Queen Njinga, "there was no remedy." Kongolese and Angolan techniques of unarmed combat were learned in the form of a martial art set in time to drum music. In short, the skills were encoded in a form of dance. Not all soldiers learned these techniques. Specialists, called *imbare* (singular *kimbare* or *quimbare*) and often drawn from slave populations, were recruited to learn the art. According to John Thornton, this specialized form of dance, called *sanga* in the Kikongo language and *sanguar* in Ndongo, valued hand-to-hand combat skills, the use of sticks and other weapons, as well as "the ability to twist, leap, and dodge to avoid arrows or the blows of opponents." The skills, which brought renown to the imbare, were displayed at public exhibitions that impressed not only Africans but Portuguese, Italian, and Dutch observers as well. Thornton notes how a Kongolese state delegation in Brazil amazed observers there with an exhibition of leaping and fighting skills in 1642.[23]

By the eighteenth century central African armies had developed mass-mobilization infantry tactics as a result of a century of civil war. The importance of sanga as a military form was waning. The Americas, however, were rife with evidence of its retention. It may often have been more important as a ritual than as a military tactic, but it may have yet had its uses in the latter arena. Ritualized stick fighting and dancing like that found in central Africa persisted all over the "new world." One of these dances, called *kalinda*, was a highlight of Caribbean slave festivals, although it was viewed ambivalently by planters. Brazilian slaves may have kept their unarmed combat skills honed in capoeira. A related martial art/dance form, *maculelê*, existed alongside capoeira in Bahia. In it two dancers used sticks called *grimas* as musical instruments and as weapons against each other, both at the same time, and to miss a beat was to receive a blow. In Cuba the Kongolese tradition of music and dance was also closely associated with military traditions. In the United States there is a tradition of "knocking and kicking." Thompson's observations about baton twirling take on wider significance here in the realm of cultural ways (as opposed to his focus on concrete expressions), for as a relative of kalinda and rara, baton twirling can be situated as part of this complex system of musical, social, religious, and military ways.²⁴

In a world where overt possession of weapons was limited or banned, the representation of social knowledge and military skills via rhythmic patterns of drumming and movement could be highly valuable. It was no coincidence that two of the most-frowned-upon activities in which a coastal lowlands slave could engage after 1740 were reading and *particular* forms of music—namely, the loudest forms: drums and horns. But in trying to control the knowledge that Africans had access to, Europeans only considered their own ways of expressing powerful knowledge. In their worries about loud signaling instruments, the planters missed the purpose of Thomas Butler's art—and many other African military ways. They even graced Butler with the moniker "famous master."

Three years after the Antigua conspiracy and six years after Thomas Butler's escape, South Carolina planters' worst nightmare came true in the form of "an intestine Enemy the most dreadful of Enemies." About twenty slaves, all sharing a common central African cultural background, "surpriz'd a Warehouse belonging to Mr. Hutchenson, at a Place called [Stono]; they there killed Mr. *Robert Bathurst* and Mr. *Gibbs*, plunder'd the House, and took a pretty many small Arms and Powder."²⁵ Unarmed, the slaves had effectively taken over a small arsenal. Guns and ammunition were no doubt their immediate aim, but how did they obtain them? Perhaps the last thing that the two armed sentries experienced was the combat version of Thomas Butler's "famous Pushing and Dancing," deadly hand-to-hand fighting tactics which the slaves were able to maintain even under the direct observation of planters who feared just such an enemy.

After arming themselves, the slaves marched southward with "Colours displayed and two Drums beating." When their ranks had swollen to between sixty and one hundred slave defectors, they stopped, still not far from Charleston, and "set to Dancing, Singing and beating Drums" for the purpose of calling more slaves to join them. This drumming, true to central African traditions, was in the form of an announcement, a signal, rather than a Kwa "language." By this time the planters had recovered sufficiently to respond with force. A pitched battle ensued in which more than twenty whites and twenty slaves were killed before the slaves scattered. Many runaways were captured and shot during the following weeks, but the insurrection was not considered quelled for at least a month.[26]

The evidence at Stono points to ways of doing battle that were not pan-African, much less universal. The manner of fighting and the indications of how power was expressed through music point to central Africa, but the expressions themselves were tailored to slavery. In line with Frazier's work, the expressions were not African, but in line with Herskovits's, the ways of expression correlated to central African ways. By shifting the focus of inquiry to the path between underlying structures and concrete cultural expressions, it becomes possible to discern how Africans from diverse regional backgrounds came to understand each other in ways that were broadly African and creolized rather than Coromantee, Mende, or Angolan.

Local planters had been quibbling relentlessly over the codification of new slave restrictions until the results of the Stono insurrection made cooperation imperative. In 1740 the new slave code was rushed through the Assembly. At the same time South Carolinians stepped up hostilities toward the Spanish in Saint Augustine, who offered freedom to any slaves who could escape there. Among its strictures, the new slave code prohibited "wooden swords and other dangerous weapons, or using or keeping of drums, horns, or other loud instruments which may call together, or give sign or notice to one another of their wicked designs or purposes." Dena Epstein has observed without elaboration that musical instruments were classed in the same category as dangerous weapons.[27] Perhaps the wooden swords were the sticks used in kalinda and maculelê. The planters' reaction, with its focus on specific material objects, underscored their lack of understanding. The new restrictions were analogous to taking pens, paper, and books from the literate. Such an action could have definite effects, but it would not render the literate population illiterate. The planters' worst (and perhaps only) fear was that of a power they clearly apprehended but had no way of comprehending.

African American drumming at Stono was an act of self-determination based on an autonomous agenda. It consisted of creolized western and central African ways of transforming a deep, perhaps universal, human belief in the pursuit of freedom (in the sense of autonomy for one's self or group) into a unique expression suited to the exigencies of American slavery. To speak only of "slave" resistance and accommodation in this case seems an odd twisting of the facts. In the case of drumming and music, the planters were the ones reacting defensively to ways not their own. Perhaps that is why Epstein claims, arguing from a different perspective, that "irrational though it may have been, the fear of drumming as a signal of insurrection persisted up to the outbreak of the Civil War."[28] Indeed, South Carolina's laws against drums stayed on the books until emancipation, and enforcement seems to have been fairly thorough. Couper's nineteenth-century ban on beating drums around the dead thus rested on something much broader than a simple religious belief. It rested on a long tradition of *European* resistance and accommodation to *African* ways. Though slavery was harsh, the planters' power was by no means absolute. The Hegelian master/slave dialectic appears a thin description since there was so much more to African identity in North America than could be encompassed by the term "slave."

Fiddles and the *Jali* Tradition

After 1740 mention of drums being played by slaves virtually disappeared from colonial records in South Carolina and Georgia. Curiously, drums seem to have been replaced by fiddles. From a single runaway violinist before the Stono uprising, the number of escaped low-country fiddlers reported in the *South Carolina Gazette* steadily increased during the years before the American Revolution and then abruptly disappeared during the war, with the next runaway fiddler not being noted until 1790.

Why was there an upsurge in runaway fiddlers? Violin playing provided slaves with access to some key aspects of planter culture. Charleston was noted as a musical center before the Revolution. Violins were instruments of high culture to the planters, and possession of a musical ensemble was a sign of status. Violinists were in demand for dances and entertainment. Well known in European folk and elite traditions, the instrument was not thought of as a threat, as drums were. In addition, slaves with experience on the instrument could be hired out, bringing extra income to their owners and occasionally to themselves.[29] Such slaves would have had access to casual conversations of the planters, no doubt sources of valuable information. More important, they would have had an amount of local mobility. Together these two job features provided key opportunities for potential runaways, opportunities that were not available to field hands.

Fiddling must be learned; the violin requires guidance, practice, and skill even to be played in tune, much less played well. How did slaves come to possess proficiency on the instrument? The skill had to be learned at some point. It is doubtful that many plantation owners would have afforded the luxury of a paid white violin tutor for a slave while at the same time losing valuable labor time. Violin lesson books did not appear in the colonies before the 1760s and were probably not widely distributed until well into the nineteenth century. Such manuals would have been incomprehensible without both musical and verbal literacy. A literate slave would more likely have possessed a religious text or hymnbook with no musical notation provided by an itinerant evangelist than an expensive and scarce violin manual.[30]

Slaves most often learned the art of fiddling from each other. An eighteenth-century description from Santo Domingo maintained: "many [slaves] are good violinists. That is the instrument they prefer. Many certainly play it only by rote, that is, they learn by themselves, imitating the sounds of a tune, or they are taught by another Negro, who explains only the position of the strings and the fingers, with no thought of notes."[31]

Novice fiddlers anywhere had to learn from someone who already knew how to play tunefully. If enslaved violinists learned from each other, then some of their knowledge must have come from Africa. The only slaving area where bowed instruments were prevalent was the Mende/western Atlantic region, the same area where the rice cultivators preferred by the coastal planters lived. This preference became even more pronounced after the Stono uprising, as central Africans were no longer desired.[32]

Information from notices on nine runaway slaves from the rice-planting region between 1730 and 1790 shows that most of them displayed some potential status marker. None, however, could be ascertained as African-born. Where were the Mende/western Atlantic violinists? Their playing and teaching took place mostly in a world that Europeans only viewed from the surface. Although low-country slave owners may have preferred Mende/western Atlantic African-born slaves over other *African* ethnicities for noncultivation jobs, American-born slaves were more generally preferred for these jobs and any others that required substantial contact with planter society. Mende violinists would not have had the same access to the valuable knowledge that noncultivation jobs provided. Furthermore, planters were less likely to know about the particular musical skills of their field hands, so even if Mende violinists ran away, their musical abilities might not turn up in the advertisements for them.

Planters found American-born, or "creolized," slaves to be more predictable than African-born slaves. They were also less prone to running away—unless, perhaps, they had acquired some useful knowledge about how to get by, as it seems the runaway fiddlers had. Having grown up on the plantations, creolized slaves were much more ingrained in the culture of that way of life than immigrant Africans could have been. They learned the music that Europeans wished them to play as easily as they learned the methods and techniques of African teachers. They undoubtedly knew more about planter ways than first-generation African immigrants did, both from the greater propinquity that their creole status was likely to provide and from the fact that plantations were the sites of their natal culture.

Expressing Anglo-American music in creolized African ways could accommodate slave and planter communities alike. For example, African-styled "jigs" and "reels" were present during the eighteenth century. A later example is seen in a recollection of youth written in 1876 by Henry W. Ravenel in which he invokes an older world that had been fading even when he was a child. He wrote of boyhood Christmas festivities at his family's South Carolina plantation home, which they had built in 1716: "The jig was an African dance, and a famous one in old times, before more refined notions began to prevail. However, it was always called for by some of the older ones who remembered its steps.... For the jig the music would be changed. The fiddle would assume a low monotonous tone, the whole tune running on three or four notes only (when it could be heard,) The stick-knocker changed his time, and beat a softer and slower measure. Indeed, only a few could give the 'knock' for proper effect."[33]

This was not only African-derived music; it was likely also a reinvention of the drum music so feared by the planters. Though the form (drumming) was banned, an underlying value of the enslaved musicians (public representation) was expressed in a new, creolized way that was simultaneously (but not synonymously) European and African. Creoles, not Africans, played these jigs. Jigs would have been strange and unfamiliar to a

Mende fiddler as much for the central African–derived dancing as for the tunes and antics of the planters. Creolization did not destroy cultures. Instead it naturalized cultural combinations that would have seemed absurd to the original bearers of the cultural practices so mixed.

The low repetitive monotone of the violin, using only three or four notes of indefinite pitch, could have easily been an encoding of a banned drum style. Throughout western and central Africa drummers play with two hands and two sticks or, most often, one hand and one stick. In the last configuration the drummer plays with one hand open and a drumstick in the other hand. By manipulating the tension of the drumhead with the open hand, a drummer could produce a number of distinct pitches that would be repeated and built up into a rhythmic pattern. Similarly, the fiddler's "three or four note" repetitive figures were played with an open left hand controlling the pitch and a stick, the bow, in the right. Bows, when bounced on a string, even respond (tactilely but not audibly) in much the same manner as sticks against drumheads. Evidence from Jamaica shows that kalinda musicians even held their fiddles as if they were drums (see fig. 3). Central Africans have many stringed instruments that are struck by sticks to produce changeable but indefinite-pitched percussive sounds. Among them are the musical bows used to accompany capoeira and another instrument shaped much like a violin with no strings, both of which can be traced to central African sources.[34]

Sometimes while a fiddler played, a second person would take a sturdy pair of straws—or in one case, knitting needles—each about eighteen inches in length, and, facing the fiddler's left shoulder, strike the strings of the violin between the fiddler's bow and his left hand. The practice of having a second musician play percussion on a stringed instrument was also prevalent in Latin America, where percussionists played on the wooden parts of guitars or "creole harps" with sticks as other players used the strings. This treatment of a single instrument as two functionally discrete instruments also has central African precedents. The "beating straws" technique has even found its way into white string band music.[35]

Again, it is the *ways*, not the instruments (nor, in the case of white string bands, even the people playing), that illustrate what is African in creole cultural situations. Both central African and

Fig. 3. *Musiciens d'un Calinda* by Pierre Eugène Du Simitière. Ink-and-wash drawing, Jamaica, c. 1760. Notice the position of the fiddler's left hand, reaching over the neck rather than under it, as if it were a drum. The bow is also more arched than most, like a Central African musical bow. Courtesy Du Simitière Collection, Library Company of Philadelphia.

Mende ways could be expressed simultaneously—in a way that Europeans understood differently as their own. The underlying value placed on music might not be an illuminating Africanism. The expression of that music on violins played with bows, hands, knitting needles, and straws was definitely original, an act of creation designed to meet the challenges of particular situations. But the *transformations* of widely held beliefs about music into innovative instrumentations can be traced to central African,

Mende, Kwa, and European ways of playing that are discernible even when thoroughly intertwined, as they were in eighteenth-century South Carolina.

While drums were banned, the violin functioned well for quietly representing African drumming traditions that were so feared, but little understood, by planters. The polymeter rhythms of banned drums were stored in the distinctive pulse of the stick knockers and the fiddler's three- or four-note rhythmic pattern. In order not to give away their purpose, the patterns were beaten softly, as the planters feared only the loudness of instruments and showed no comprehension of the music's other ways of representing power.

The jig, when danced by whites, was done in pairs and took place in the center of a ring of people. A woman would enter the ring, doing a shuffling dance while gracefully waving a handkerchief over her head, and a man, in Ravenel's words, would follow with "his whole soul and body thrown into the dance. The feet moved about in the most grotesque manner. . . . It was hard work, and at intervals of five or ten minutes, he was relieved by another jumping into the ring with a shout and shuffling him out."[36] The mock-confrontational shout of the entering male and his "shuffling" of the other man out of the ring again evoke the ritualized combat of capoeira and the image of Thomas Butler's pushing and dancing. Perhaps the slave would have enjoyed the irony that these pushing and dancing *masters* unknowingly imitated the most deadly aspect of the music they sought to ban.

Obviously, violins did not simply substitute for drums in the years following the Stono uprising. Creolized fiddling had a different set of capabilities for representation than did drums. Stringed instruments, whether bowed or plucked, were part of the *jali* (griot) tradition, which existed throughout the slaving regions of Africa, but generated from a hearth area in the Mende/western Atlantic regions, whereas the court drumming traditions were most developed further south, in the Kwa and Kongo/Angolan regions. Thus the playing of jigs and reels on a classical European instrument, the violin, represented roots that simultaneously led back to northern, western, and central sub-Saharan Africa as well as Europe.

The court tradition, which manifested itself in the drumming and dancing that so intimidated planters, was a means of directly representing and displaying power. Drummers and dancers were agents representing an immanent fighting or political force. The meaning of the drumming message was known only to insiders, though outsiders apprehended its power. Court drumming was an ephemeral, instantaneous means of mass communication and representation, perhaps the original form of broadcasting. Like a voice, as soon as the representation is uttered it is gone. But also like a voice, its expressive power extends beyond the semantic content of the words alone.

Whereas court music represented power, jali songs described and explained it. The music of the jali tradition, to continue the analogy with other media, is more like a text. It is an editable, manipulable, analyzable medium that can be recalled in the same form. The songs were not documents of the past so much as means of encoding information. Usually what they encoded was some sort of legitimation of, or recipe for, power and its use. Violins were used as a jali form of storing powerful traditions, namely, court drumming patterns and the rhythms of military dance. These stored forms could be reconstituted as direct manifestations of power. They were an effective way of transmitting knowledge across time.

"Turkish" Military Music in the Revolution

Descriptions of music during the American Revolution show that slaves from the coastal lowlands were able to maintain their aptitudes for drumming throughout the three and a half decades since it had been prohibited. The number of runaway African drummers from South Carolina noted in print boomed from one during the previous forty years to twenty between 1775 and 1780. All were Charleston slaves; and all but one, the "Negro Bob" who drummed for the South Carolina revolutionaries, joined Hessian regiments that promised freedom in exchange for military service. At least eighty-two people from the colonies joined the Hessian forces during the Revolution. Of these eighty-two, fifty-two were drummers, and thirty-five of the latter were black. Twenty-seven of the recruits, or about one-third of the total, were from the Charleston plantation area. Twenty-four of the Charleston recruits were black, nineteen of whom were employed as drummers, two as fifers, and three as laborers. Only one of the Hessians could be identified as African-born.[37]

Military drummers for the American revolutionaries were drawn from the rank and file. Their drumming was used mostly for sending field directions and was in a state of disarray for much of the war. No particular facility on the drums was required to become a military drummer for the revolutionary forces. The main task was to send loud, simple coded instructions by means of rudimentary drum patterns. If Hessian troops had operated under the same standards as the revolutionaries, the reason for the large number of African drummers joining them could simply be written off as an interest in doing something that had been previously prohibited.[38]

Europeans, however, considered German military bands to be the best in the world from the 1750s until the turn of the century. German military units were participants in the craze for Janissary music, which had been slowly sweeping westward through Europe from 1720 onward. However, the British did not adopt the style until the 1790s. During the American Revolution, English regiments continued with traditional fife-and-drum field units and hautbois military bands as the norms. The skill requirements for drumming in such a corps were not much different from those for American drummers.[39] This provides an explanation for why men skilled in African drumming traditions found such ready positions in Hessian rather than English or American regiments.

In theory, the Janissary style favored by the Hessians was derived from Turkish military music. Instruments used included several large drums, tambourines, and high-pitched flutes and reeds. But Europeans confronted Janissary music not in alliance, but as enemies, so the borrowing was often secondhand. In Germany, Africans became the preferred musicians for Janissary corps, especially as drummers. They were acclaimed as such and changed the drumming pattern from the Turkish form to what a regimental leader labeled "modern cross-handed drumming." They were dressed flamboyantly, and their marching was a stylized form of cadenced dance that drew on the same sources as kalinda, rara, and baton twirling. It involved leaping and contortions as well as the throwing and catching of drumsticks and the adroit handling of batons and jangled sticks, all skills maintained by the culturally conditioned transformations of Africans' military values. Regiments would compete to have the best and wildest Janissary units.[40] Virtuoso skill was a requirement and could not be had on short notice. It took years of practice. It was exactly these roles that creole Africans from the low country stepped into when they joined Hessian forces.

The parallels between the Janissary performance and the violin music described above include stick work, agile dancing, rhythmic virtuosity, and strict adherence to time. The similarities to African forms of court and military music include all of the above plus the court function of immediate representation. Much like Kwa court music, Janissary regimental performances communicated an immanent force. This function was in marked contrast to the jali-like performances of African American fiddlers. But without the encoded "text" or "recipes" that were stored and represented in jigs and fiddling, creolized enslaved Africans would have been less likely to fill spots as Hessian drummers when the opportunities arose to "read these texts aloud" as displays of a present power.

Conclusions

The Revolution had disastrous effects on planter society in the coastal lowlands. The region from Savannah to Charleston was lost to British and Hessian forces in the worst defeats of the war for the revolutionaries. Plantations were plundered, families fled, and slaves escaped during the conquest and occupation of the rice-growing districts. Coastal rice-growing society, and the institution of slavery that supported it, never fully recovered from the effects of the Revolutionary War. Slavery itself was becoming an institution under siege. In 1808 the importation of slaves was banned. Although some Africans were still imported illegally, the nineteenth century saw the completion of Africans' transition from enslavement in America to membership in an African American society largely bound in slavery. During this period African ways of representing the world mingled inextricably with each other and with European-American culture. The roles of African American women changed as they suddenly became the primary remaining source for new slaves as well as being the main source for transmission of cultural ways to the last enslaved generations.

The cultural expression of power through music began to take new forms. The creolized rhythms of jigs and reels found their way into work songs and the clapped accompaniments to spirituals. With its message of equality, the religion of revivals was immensely attractive to slaves and offered a new forum for seeking freedom. Spirituals provided a major vehicle for expressing this power both within and against the confines of slavery. Like fiddling, this expression was not always in opposition to European culture. Parallels between the two cultures opened up the spaces where enslaved African Americans could frame and pursue autonomous agendas with the least amount of resistance from Anglo-Americans.

There was more cultural space available to African culture in the low country and elsewhere in the Americas than existed within the institutional confines of slavery. Their world was not only in resistance to or accommodation of the slaveholders, even though from the planters' perspective it might have seemed to be. A close study of what the planters were themselves unconscious reveals that the world they thought they owned was not always as it appeared to them.

African culture in the Americas was more than simply a reaction to bondage, but it was not a simple transfer of the "African" to "America" either. Mende fiddling and jali ways, Kwa-based court drumming and tone languages, central African martial arts and percussion instruments, European-derived music and dance—all could be woven together seamlessly within a single expression uniquely suited to an American context, whether in pushing and dancing, jigs and reels, "Janissary music," or Sea Island spirituals. Focusing on synchronic transformations of beliefs into expressions allows glimpses of this creolizing world even through the distorted lens left by planters' records. The stories of how these transformations changed over time provide us with keys not only to the history of African American identities, but to all the many American identities that have long struggled both to comprise and pull apart the very notion of "America."

Music is only one means of representing an internal world externally, albeit one which has left a substantial record. The study of cultural transformations, or ways, can be applied to other domains as well, yielding new insights into cultures poorly represented by few or biased textual sources. Religious, agricultural, and economic practices could all be approached this way. The concept of transforming an underlying belief or value into a specific, historically discernible manifestation offers a means of understanding how people from different cultural backgrounds negotiated their realities—literally, how they made sense of their worlds. It also offers a means of filtering out some biases in source materials, as these cultural indicators were often manifested unconsciously and left traces in documents in ways that can be teased out even in the face of severe prejudices and omissions.

Scholars will still argue over whether or not slavery destroyed America's African past. To answer the question would spoil the sport. But the bigger issues lie in how to explain a society in which two seemingly paradoxical scenarios are possible. Could any culture (African or European) survive the ordeal of slavery unchanged? Did slavery have the ability to destroy anyone's culture completely? The Herskovits-Frazier problem has been resolved, and for creole cultures the answer to the question of who is right is, of course, "both and neither." Rather than trying to reduce the answer, this article has sought to explain a small part of *how* such a paradox has come to exist. In doing so, a space opens in which it becomes possible to inquire *for what* such a creolized African past was used.

Notes

Pete Daniel, Monisha Das Gupta, Dennis Downey, David Hackett Fischer, Linda Heywood, Judith Irvine, Howard Johnson, Patrick Manning, Peter Seitel, Kenneth Shields, Ibrahim Sundiata, John Thornton, Chris Warren, and Peter Wood provided suggestions, encouragement, cautions, and guidance during this essay's long gestation. I benefitted from lively discussions of various versions and portions of this work at the World History Seminar at Northeastern University, the conference on "Creole Cultures in Latin America and the Caribbean" at the University of Delaware, the Society for Pidgin and Creole Linguistics, the Southern Historical Society, and with my colleagues and students at Oberlin College and Hamilton College. Time to think and write came from an Ira and Rose Crown Fellowship at Brandeis University and a research fellowship at the Smithsonian Institution.

1. For a study of cultural creolization that distinguishes pidginization and creolization from each other and from related processes, see Richard Cullen Rath, "African Music in Seventeenth-Century Jamaica: Cultural Transit and Transition," *William and Mary Quarterly* 50 (Oct., 1993): 700–26. For the demographic, historical, and linguistic factors defining creolization, see Phillip Baker and Chris Corne, "Universals, Substrata and the Indian Ocean Creoles," in *Substrata Versus Universals in Creole Genesis: Papers from the Amsterdam Creole Workshop, April 1985*, ed. Pieter Muysken and Norval Smith (Amsterdam and Philadelphia: J. Benjamins, 1986), pp. 165–67; Jeff Siegel, *Language Contact in a Plantation Environment: A Sociolinguistic History of Fiji* (Cambridge and New York: Cambridge University Press, 1987), p. 16; Ronald Wardaugh, *An Introduction to Sociolinguistics*, 2d ed. (Oxford: Blackwell, 1992), p. 59; Derek Bickerton, *Roots of Language* (Ann Arbor: Karoma, 1981), pp. 2–4;

Derek Bickerton, *Language & Species* (Chicago: University of Chicago Press, 1990), pp. 105–29; John Holm, *Pidgins and Creoles*, vol. 1 (Cambridge and New York: Cambridge University Press, 1988), p. 6; Peter Mühlhäusler, *Pidgin and Creole Linguistics* (Oxford and New York: Blackwell, 1986), p. 8; Richard Cullen Rath, "Creolization Hypertext Project" (unpublished software, in author's possession).

2. Noam Chomsky, *Syntactic Structures* (Paris: Mouton, 1957). The most accessible (and entertaining) history of generative grammar is Randy Allen Harris, *The Linguistics Wars* (New York: Oxford University Press, 1993). The structuralist (i.e., pregenerative grammar) approach to transformations is best represented by Chomsky's mentor, Zellig Harris. See Zellig Harris, *Methods in Structural Linguistics* (Chicago: University of Chicago Press, 1951); Zellig Harris, *Papers in Structural and Transformational Linguistics* (Dordrecht: Reidel, 1970). Important programmatic shifts in generative grammar are marked in Noam Chomsky, *Aspects of the Theory of Syntax* (Cambridge: M.I.T. Press, 1965); Noam Chomsky, *Rules and Representations* (New York: Columbia University Press, 1980); and Noam Chomsky, *A Minimalist Program for Linguistic Theory*, M.I.T. occasional papers in linguistics, no. 1 (Cambridge: M.I.T. Working Papers in Linguistics, 1992), esp. pp. 1–8. The last describes the approach to linguistic transformations implicit in this article.

3. On "languages" and "communities" as unruly objects of study that are undefinable in any but fuzzy terms, see William Labov, "Is There a Creole Speech Community?," in *Theoretical Orientations in Creole Studies*, ed. Albert Valdman and Arnold Highfield (New York: Academy Press, 1980), pp. 369–70, 382, 384–85; Noam Chomsky, *Knowledge of Language: Its Nature, Origin, and Use* (New York: Praeger Scientific, 1986), pp. 18–36, esp. p. 25; W. N. Francis, *Dialectology, An Introduction* (London and New York: Longman, 1983), pp. 1–7; Frank Parker, *Linguistics for Non-Linguists* (Austin: Pro-ed, 1986), p. 115; and Lawrence M. Davis, *English Dialectology, An Introduction* (University: University of Alabama Press, 1983), pp. 1–3. For the importance of the Wittgensteinian ideas of fuzzy sets and "private languages," see Eleanor Rosch and Carolyn B. Mervis, "Family Resemblances: Studies in the Internal Structures of Categories," *Cognitive Psychology* 7 (1975): 573–603; Saul A. Kripke, *Wittgenstein on Rules and Private Language: An Elementary Exposition* (Cambridge, Mass.: Harvard University Press, 1982); and Noam Chomsky, "Explaining Language Use," *Philosophical Topics* 20 (spring, 1992): 205–32.

4. Jack P. Greene, *Pursuits of Happiness: The Social Development of Early Modern British Colonies and the Formation of American Culture* (Chapel Hill: University of North Carolina Press, 1988); Benedict Anderson, *Imagined Communities: Reflections of the Origin and Spread of Nationalism*, rev. ed. (London and New York: Verso, 1991); Edward Brathwaite, *The Development of Creole Society in Jamaica, 1770–1820* (Oxford: Clarendon Press, 1971); Edouard Glissant, *Caribbean Discourse: Selected Essays*, tr. J. Michael Dash (Charlottesville: University Press of Virginia, 1989). Linguistic models are discussed below.

5. W. E. B. Du Bois, review of *Life and Labor in the Old South* by Ulrich Bonnell Phillips, in *Book Reviews by W. E. B. Dubois*, ed. Herbert Aptheker (Millwood, N.Y.: KTO Press, 1977); E. Franklin Frazier, *The Negro Family in the United States* (1939; Chicago: University of Chicago Press, 1948); Melville J. Herskovits, *The Myth of the Negro Past* (1941; Boston: Beacon Press, 1958). On Du Bois's synthesis of the "loss" and "persistence" approaches, see Richard Cullen Rath, "Echo and Narcissus: The Afrocentric Pragmatism of W. E. B. Du Bois," *Journal of American History* 84 (Sept., 1997): 492–93 n. 74.

6. Stanley M. Elkins, *Slavery: A Problem in American Institutional and Intellectual Life* (Chicago: University of Chicago Press, 1959); Kenneth M. Stampp, *The Peculiar Institution: Slavery in the Ante-Bellum South* (New York: Vintage Books, 1956); Daniel Patrick Moynihan, *Social and Economic Conditions of Negroes in the United States*, Bureau of Labor Statistics and Bureau of the Census, BLS Rpt. no. 332 and Current Population Reports, Series P-23, no. 24 (Washington, D.C.: Government Printing Office, 1976); Eugene D. Genovese, *Roll, Jordan, Roll: The World the Slaves Made* (New York: Random House, 1974).

7. John W. Blassingame, *The Slave Community: Plantation Life in the Antebellum South* (1972; Oxford: Oxford University Press, 1979); Herbert George Gutman, *The Black Family in Slavery and Freedom, 1750–1925* (New York: Vintage Books, 1976).

8. Sidney Mintz and Richard Price, *Birth of African-American Culture: An Anthropological Perspective* (1976; Boston: Beacon Press, 1992), pp. 9–10, 20–21, 52–53.

9. Barbara Kopytoff, "The Development of Jamaican Maroon Ethnicity," *Caribbean Quarterly* 22 (1976): 33–50; Albert J. Raboteau, *Slave Religion: The "Invisible Institution" in the Antebellum South* (Oxford: Oxford University Press, 1978); Daniel C. Littlefield, *Rice and Slaves: Ethnicity and the Slave Trade in Colonial South Carolina* (Baton Rouge: Louisiana State University Press, 1981); Charles W. Joyner, *Down by the Riverside: A South Carolina Slave Community* (Urbana: University of Illinois Press, 1985); Patricia Jones-Jackson, *When Roots Die: Endangered Traditions on the Sea Islands* (Athens: University of Georgia Press, 1987); John Michael Vlach, *By the Work of Their Hands: Studies in Afro-American Folklife* (Charlottesville: University Press of Virginia, 1991); Michael Mullin, *Africa in America* (Urbana: University of Illinois Press, 1992); Roger D. Abrahams, *Singing the Master: The Emergence of African American Culture in the Plantation South* (New York: Random House, 1992); and Ira Berlin, "From Creole to African: Atlantic Creoles and the Origins of African-American in Mainland North America," *William and Mary Quarterly* 53 (July, 1996): 251–88. Berlin has redefined "creole" to refer to successful African and African American cultural brokers or intercultural mediators. For strong substratist positions see Winifred Vass, *The Bantu Speaking Heritage of the United States* (Los Angeles: Center for Afro-American Studies, University of California, 1979); Joseph E. Holloway, ed., *Africanisms in American Culture* (Bloomington and Indianapolis: University of Indiana Press, 1990); and Gwendolyn Midlo Hall, *Africans in Colonial Louisiana: The Development of Afro-Creole Culture in the Eighteenth Century* (Baton Rouge: Louisiana State University Press, 1992). For critiques of Mintz and Price, see John Thornton, *Africa and Africans in the Making of the Atlantic World, 1400–1680* (Cambridge: Cambridge University Press, 1992), pp. 183–234; Rath, "African Music in Seventeenth-Century Jamaica"; Douglas B. Chambers, "'He Is an African But Speaks Plain': Historical Creolization in Eighteenth-Century Virginia," in *The African Diaspora*, ed. Alusine Jalloh and Stephen E. Maizlish (College Station: Texas A&M University Press, 1996), pp. 100–33; and Paul E. Lovejoy, "The African Diaspora: Revisionist Interpretations of Ethnicity, Culture and Religion under Slavery," *Studies in the World History of Slavery, Abolition and Emancipation* 2, no. 1 (1997): <http://www.h-net.msu.edu/~slavery/essays/esy9701love.html>. Lovejoy interprets Mintz and Price as arguing against African culture being transferred to the Americas even though the issue of how African cultures were transformed in the process of creating African American culture is central to their thesis. Lovejoy compounds the confusion by having Mintz and Price's synthesis of Herskovits and Frazier stand for a "creoliza-

tion school" of historians who reject the idea of an African substrate. Most historians using creolization as a model tacitly reject Mintz and Price's synthesis for a stronger substratist approach much like the one Lovejoy proposes as an alternative to creolization.

10. Mintz and Price, *Birth of African-American Culture*, p. 46, emphasis in original. For a discussion of "near" universals, a subset of "statistical" universals, see Donald E. Brown, *Human Universals* (New York: McGraw-Hill, 1991), pp. 42–45.

11. For more on *rara*, see Leslie G. Desmangles, *The Faces of the Gods: Vodon and Roman Catholicism in Haiti* (Chapel Hill: University of North Carolina Press, 1992), pp. 57, 193–94. Thompson draws upon and extends the work of Szwed. See Robert Farris Thompson, "Kongo Influences on African-American Artistic Culture," in *Africanisms in American Culture*, ed. Holloway, pp. 161–62, 182*nn* 59, 60.

12. The fairest, most accessible evaluation of the various theories of creole genesis is in Wardaugh, *Introduction to Sociolinguistics*, pp. 72–77. For Bickerton's theories see Bickerton, *Roots of Language*; Bickerton, *Language & Species*, pp. 105–29; and Derek Bickerton, "Creole Languages," *Scientific American* 249 (1983): 116–21. For debates between Bickerton and the substratists, see Pieter Muysken and Norval Smith, eds., *Substrata Versus Universals in Creole Genesis: Papers from the Amsterdam Creole Workshop, April 1985* (Amsterdam and Philadelphia: J. Benjamins, 1986) or any issue of the *Journal of Pidgin and Creole Linguistics*.

13. The single exception is Frances Karttunen and Alfred W. Crosby, "Language Death, Language Genesis, and World History," *Journal of World History* 6, no. 2 (1995): 157–74. Gwendolyn Midlo Hall mentions but dismisses Bickerton in Hall, *Africans in Colonial Louisiana*. See also Steven Pinker, *The Language Instinct* (New York: W. Morrow and Co., 1994). Pinker, a cognitive scientist studying the origins of language, essentializes culture as an innate faculty analogous to the language endowment (rather than integrally connected to it). By doing so, he is able to posit a number of putative cultural universals that suspiciously resemble Eurocentric opinions.

14. Georgia Writers Project, *Drums and Shadows: Survival Studies among the Georgia Coastal Negroes* (1940; Athens: University of Georgia Press, 1986), p. 180; Lydia Parrish, *Slave Songs of the Georgia Sea Islands* (1942; Athens: University of Georgia Press, 1992). Johnson's words were written as "he use tuh beat duh drum tuh duh fewnul, but Mr Couper he stop dat. He say he dohn wahn drums beatin roun duh dead." I have paraphrased in order to defer issues of dialect misrepresentation. See Edgar W. Schneider, *American Earlier Black English: Morphological and Syntactical Variables* (Tuscaloosa: University of Alabama Press, 1989), pp. 1–16, 42–53. Slaves' names often reflected their places of origin or where they were purchased. The Ndembu, or Dembo, area of central Africa comprised a politically unstable periphery of the Kingdom of Kongo, making Dembo most likely a captive imported from that region. For Ndembu, see Thornton, *Africa and Africans*, pp. xxxi–xxxiii. For naming a slave after a region, see Newbell Niles Puckett, "Names of American Negro Slaves," in *Motherwit from the Laughing Barrel: Readings in the Interpretation of Afro-American Folklore*, ed. Alan Dundes (New York: Garland Publishing, 1981), p. 159. For Couper, see Malcom Bell, Jr., *Major Butler's Legacy* (Athens: University of Georgia Press, 1987), p. 398. Couper lived until 1866, managing the family's plantation. His sons were both killed in the Civil

War, and his father had died in 1850, before Johnson was born. Thus, Dembo was most likely drumming while he was enslaved.

15. Girolamo Merolla, *A Voyage to Congo and Several Other Countries, Chiefly in Southern-Africk*, in *A Collection of Voyages and Travels*, vol. 1, ed. Awnsham Churchill (1682; London: Printed for A. and J. Churchill, 1704), pp. 651–756. For Songo, see Thornton, *Africa and Africans*, p. xxxv.

16. Dena Epstein, *Sinful Tunes and Spirituals: Black Folk Music to the Civil War* (Urbana and Chicago: University of Illinois Press, 1977), pp. 58–60, 62.

17. On the uses of drums for displays of state power, particularly in Kwa regions, see T. Edward Bowditch, "Excerpts from *Mission from Cape Coast Castle to Asshantee*," in *Readings in Black American Music*, ed. Eileen Southern (1819; New York: Norton, 1983), pp. 9–15; J. H. Kwabena Nketia, "History and Organization of Music in West Africa," in *Essays on Music and History in Africa*, ed. Klaus Wachsmann (Evanston: Northwestern University Press, 1971), pp. 17–22; J. H. Kwabena Nketia, *African Music in Ghana* (Evanston: Northwestern University Press, 1963), pp. 47–48, 103; J. H. Kwabena Nketia, *The Music of Africa* (New York: W. W. Norton, 1974), pp. 167–70; Meki Nzewi, "Traditional Strategies for Mass Communication: The Centrality of Igbo Music," in *Selected Reports in Ethnomusicology*, vol. 5 (Los Angeles: University of California Press, 1984), pp. 318–28; R. S. Rattray, *Akan-Ashanti Folk-Tales* (Oxford: Clarendon Press, 1930), pp. 133–34. Kwa languages are spoken from the Ibo region of eastern Nigeria to the westernmost area of present-day Ghana. According to glottochronologists, a single Kwa language began to fragment about eight thousand years ago, and now the eastern and western language branches are only marginally related. All of then are tonemic, however, with Yoruba speakers, at the center, using nine tones. To the west of this tonal "hearth," western Kwa languages generally have two to four tones. See William E. Welmers, *African Language Structures* (Berkeley: University of California Press, 1973).

18. *Records in the British Public Records Office*, trans. 13, p. 196; *South Carolina Commons House Journals*, 1702, pp. 64–65 and 1707–1708, p. 53, all cited in Peter Wood, *Black Majority: Negroes in Colonial South Carolina from 1670 through the Stono Rebellion* (New York: Norton, 1975), p. 125.

19. For the Charleston "conspiracy," see *Pennsylvania Gazette*, Oct. 29–Nov. 5, 1730; and *Boston Weekly Newsletter*, Oct. 22, 1730 (cited in Wood, *Black Majority*, p. 299). The letter itself was dated Aug. 20, 1730, in both papers. For a general account of Antigua, see David Barry Gaspar, *Bondmen and Rebels: A Study of Master-Slave Relations in Antigua* (Baltimore: Johns Hopkins University Press, 1985). While drumming was not an issue at the actual inquest, the fact that it was reported so in the North American press underscores Anglo-American elites' fears in this regard. See *Pennsylvania Gazette*, Mar. 10–17, 1737, and Mar. 17–24, 1737.

20. Joseph E. Holloway, "The Origins of African-American Culture," in *Africanisms in American Culture*, ed. Holloway, pp. 4–11; Wood, *Black Majority*, pp. 334–39; Littlefield, *Rice and Slaves*, pp. 109–35.

21. *South Carolina Gazette*, May 19–May 26, 1733. See Wood, *Black Majority*, pp. 244–45 for remarks on Vander Dussen's (also spelled as Vanderdussen) temperament.

22. For capoeira, see John Storm Roberts, *Black Music of Two Worlds* (New York: Praeger Publishers, 1972), pp. 27–28; and John Lowell Lewis, *Ring of Libera-*

tion: *Deceptive Discourse in Brazilian Capoeira* (Chicago: University of Chicago Press, 1992). For musical bows, see Jos Gansemans and Barbara Schmidt-Wrenger, *Zentralafrika: Musikgeschichte in Bildern* (Leipzig: VEB Deutscher Verlag für Musik, 1986), pp. 127–31; Gerhard Kubik, "Capoeira Angola and Berimbau," in *Angolan Traits in Black Music Games and Dances of Brazil: A Study of African Cultural Extensions Overseas* (Lisbon: Junta de Investigacoes Cientificas do Ultramar, 1976), pp. 27–36.

23. John K. Thornton, "The Art of War in Angola," *Comparative Studies in Society and Culture* 30 (Apr., 1988): 362–65.

24. For kalinda see Roberts, *Black Music of Two Worlds*, pp. 26–27, 115–16, 123, 157; and Epstein, *Sinful Tunes and Spirituals*, pp. 24, 28, 30–38, 82, 92, 94, 135. For batons see Thompson, "Kongo Influences on African-American Artistic Culture," pp. 162–63, 182–83. For Cuba see Odilio Urfe, "Music and Dance in Cuba," in *Africa in Latin America*, ed. Manuel Moreno Fraginals (New York: Holmes & Meier, 1984), pp. 170–88, esp. pp. 173, 176, 181, 183, 185. For "knocking and kicking" see G. Daniel Dawson's liner notes in Grupo de Capoeira Angola Pelourinho, *Capoeira Angola: Salvador, Brazil*, sound recording (Washington D.C.: Folkways/Smithsonian, 1996). For maculelê see Bira Almeida, *Capoeira, a Brazilian Art Form: History, Philosophy, and Practice* (Berkeley: North Atlantic Books, 1986), pp. 46–47n 8, 159.

25. "Extract of a Letter from South Carolina Dated October 2," *Gentleman's Magazine* 10 (1740): 127–29, cited in Michael Mullin, ed., *American Negro Slavery: A Documentary History* (Columbia: University of South Carolina Press, 1976), p. 85; *South Carolina Commons House Journals* (1739–41; Columbia, S.C.: 1907–46, 1951–62), p. 84, cited in Wood, *Black Majority*, p. 321; "Account of the Negroe Insurrection in South Carolina," in *Colonial Records of the State of Georgia*, vol. 23, ed. Allan D. Chandler and Lucien L. Knights (Atlanta, 1904–16), p. 233, cited in Wood, *Black Majority*, pp. 314–20.

26. Peter Wood refers to the twenty slaves who formed the core of the revolt as "Angolans"; See Wood, *Black Majority*, p. 314. John Thornton presents military, contextual, and religious evidence indicating that the core group was from the closely related Kingdom of Kongo. John K. Thornton, "African Dimensions of the Stono Rebellion," *American Historical Review* 46 (1991): 1101–13.

27. Wood, *Black Majority;* South Carolina, *The Statues at Large: South Carolina*, vol. 8, ed. Thomas Cooper and David J. McCord (Columbia: A. S. Johnston, 1840), p. 410; *A Codification of the Statute Law of Georgia, Including the English Statutes of Force*, ed. William A. Hotchkiss (Savannah: J. M. Cooper, 1845), p. 813, all cited in Epstein, *Sinful Tunes and Spirituals*, pp. 59, 60, 62.

28. Epstein, *Sinful Tunes and Spirituals*, p. 60.

29. For musicians as status symbols to planters and Charleston as a musical center, see Raoul F. Camus, *Military Music of the American Revolution* (Chapel Hill: University of North Carolina Press, 1976), pp. 54–55. For the demand for slave musicians see Tilford Brooks, *America's Black Musical Heritage* (Englewood Cliffs, N.J.: Prentice-Hall, 1984), pp. 164–68. For "hiring out" see Epstein, *Sinful Tunes and Spirituals*, p. 80.

30. The earliest extant American violin manual is Francesco Geminiani's *An Abstract of Geminiani's Art of Playing on the Violin* (Boston: John Boyles, 1769), pp. 1, 5–6, 10. The only extant copy is bound from three or four partial sets of pages that had been combined to make a single thirteen-page volume

(thanks to Daniel Slive for interpreting the binding and paper). The John Carter Brown Library purchased that copy from a British bookseller. Not all the musical notation is printed either, indicating that the Boston printers may have been unable to deliver the pamphlet to market at all. A 1763 advertisement in Newport, Rhode Island, announced, "Crone's Rules to play the Fiddle Well, without a Master, by Way of Question and Answer, with 25 copper Plates." See LaBrew, *Black Musicians of the Colonial Period: Preliminary Index* ([Detroit]: [LaBrew], 1981), p. 12. Both manuals seem to have been aimed at New Englanders rather than southern African American readers, though. On what slaves might be likely to read, see Samuel Davies, *The State of Religion in Virginia, Particularly among the Negroes*, 2d ed. (London: R. Pardon, 1757).

31. Moreau de Saint-Méry, Médéric Louis Élie, *Déscription Topographique, Physique, Civile, Politique, and Historique de la Partie Française de l'Isle Saint-Dominigue*, vol. 1 (Philadelphia: Chez l'Auteur, 1797), p. 51. The "rough translation" of the cited passage into English is made by Epstein, *Sinful Tunes and Spirituals*, p. 116.

32. For increased imports from Mende/western Atlantic groups after Stono see Creel, *"Peculiar People."*

33. Henry William Ravenel, "Recollections of Southern Plantation Life," *Yale Review* 26 (June, 1936): 768–69; also 750, 774–75. Also see Epstein, *Sinful Tunes and Spirituals*, pp. 77–87, 114–17, 120–24.

34. The pattern of drummers holding a stick in one hand (most often the right one) is found throughout western and central Africa. It is most pronounced north of the Kongo/Angola region. In the Kongo/Angola region playing with two hands—or, less often, with two sticks—predominates, but playing with one hand, one stick is not uncommon either. For seventeenth-century visual evidence of this, see the reproductions in Gerhard Kubik, *Westafrika: Musikgeschicte in Bildern*, vol. 11 (Leipzig: VEB Deutscher Verlag für Musik, 1989), pp. 47, 49, 67, 69, 73, 79, 84, 99, 113, 114; and Gansemans and Schmidt-Wrenger, *Zentralafrika*, pp. 17, 19, 51, 62, 68, 71, 95, 99, 108, 123, 165–67. For stringless violin-shaped instruments played with a stick see Giovanni Antonio Cavazzi, *Istorica Descrizione de' tre' Regni Congo, Matamba et Angola* (Bologna: Per Giacomo Monti, 1687), p. 200. Many illustrations from both can be found in Gansemans and Schmidt-Wrenger, *Zentralafrika*, pp. 15–27, 127–31.

35. David C. Barrow, "A Georgia Corn Shucking," *Century Magazine* 24 (1882): 878, cited in Roger D. Abrahams, *Singing the Master: The Emergence of African American Culture in the Plantation South* (New York: Random House, 1992), pp. 103n 40, 186; Nettie Powell, *A History of Marion County, Georgia* (Columbus, Ga.: Historical Publishing Company, 1931), p. 33, cited in Abrahams, *Singing the Master*, p. 186; William C. Handy, *Father of the Blues* (New York: Macmillan, 1941), p. 5, cited in Abrahams, *Singing the Master*, pp. 103n 40, 186. For the prevalence of related practices in Latin America and the Caribbean, see Isabel Aretz, "Music and Dance in Continental Latin America, with the Exception of Brazil," in *Africa in Latin America*, ed. Manuel Moreno Fraginals (New York: Holmes & Meier, 1984), p. 197. For "beating straws" in Anglo-American fiddling in Alabama, see Joyce H. Cauthen, *With Fiddle and Well-Rosined Bow: Old-time Fiddling in Alabama* (Tuscaloosa: University of Alabama Press, 1989).

36. Ravenel, "Recollections of Southern Plantation Life," pp. 768–69. The ring and the shuffling step and their implications as pan-Africanisms are dis-

cussed at length in Stuckey, *Slave Culture: Nationalist Theory and the Foundations of Black America* (New York: Oxford University Press, 1986). Thornton (personal communication, Mar. 10, 1993) has found similar accounts of this behavior as depicted by Italian missionaries to Kongo in the 1690s. See Marcellino d'Atri, *L'anarchia congolese*, fol. 335 of the original MS (p. 158 of Carlo Tosso's edition) and Luca da Caltanisetta's MS, fol. 60 (p. 290 of Romain Rainero's edition). Neither of these accounts describes military displays, but the functional divide between forms of entertainment and forms of training may not have existed.

37. Compiled from LaBrew, *Index of Black Musicians from the Colonial Period*, pp. 115–22. The author lists two men, Prince Lewis and Ketto, among the Hessian recruits whose races were unknown. The names "Prince" and "Cato" were almost exclusively used among slaves, so these two were listed as being of African descent in the compiled totals.

38. For American military drumming see Camus, *Military Music of the American Revolution*, pp. 8–9, 128–50; also see Eileen Southern, *The Music of Black Americans: A History*, 2d ed. (New York: Norton, 1983), p. 65.

39. Henry George Farmer, *The Rise and Development of Military Music* (1912; Freeport, N.Y.: Books for Libraries Press, 1970), frontispiece and pp. 66, 70–78; Camus, *Military Music of the American Revolution*, pp. 35–39, 122; LaBrew, *Black Musicians of the Colonial Period*, in which appear between pp. 122 and 123 three foldout contemporary illustrations of members of Hessian regiments who served in the American war. All three depict African drummers. See also LaBrew, *Black Musicians of the Colonial Period*, pp. 99–122.

40. Henry G. Farmer, "The Turkish Influence in Military Music," in *Handel's Kettledrums and Other Papers on Military Music* (London: Hinrichsen Edition, Ltd, 1950), p. 46, cited in Raoul F. Camus, "The Military Band in the United States Army Prior to 1834" (Ph.D. diss., New York University, 1969), p. 130.

The Evidence for Pidgin/Creolization in Early American English

J. L. Dillard

Despite widespread acceptance of the existence of Gullah ("Geechee") and Louisiana French creole, there has been a great deal of resistance to the idea of extensive creolization in American English, specifically in the history of the dialect variously known as black English, African American vernacular English, or "Ebonics." Even in the field of creole studies there is dissension. First considered—in Labov's monumental but not absolutely perfect study of social variation—as identical with working-class white dialect, at least in New York City, the variety was approached under the cover of association with Puerto Rican English and then variously accounted for. The creolist hypothesis has perhaps been the most hotly debated. Since it has proved impossible to establish identity of the black or African American dialect with regional dialects familiarized in the Linguistic Atlas of the United States and Canada project, G. Bailey, among others, has proclaimed that the differences are of recent origin.[1]

There are, however, many attestations to the existence of early (especially eighteenth-century) pidginized or creolized varieties. They have been cited endlessly, and the addition of more examples—easy as they are to find—would not convince those linguists who insist that all these are linguistic fakery. That seems to be the thrust of George Krapp's pioneering chapter on "Literary Dialects," and the notion spread fairly quickly through the academic community, coming even to such modest levels as the master's thesis.[2] To insist that such attestors as Cotton Mather, Benjamin Franklin, Hugh Henry Brackenridge, Associate Justice Daniel P. Horsmanden, and even Frederick Douglass had little contact with each other and no cause to be members of the same controversy proves to be of no use. Neither has it been effective to point out that these and many others who recorded examples of black English far earlier than the Civil War have no apparent biasing factor to complicate their use as evidence.³

Edgar Schneider, on totally a priori grounds, rejects the theory of a pidgin utilized by West Africans who fell victim to the slave trade. In 1989 he wrote: "Dillard and his followers assume that enslaved Africans were taught pidgin English in the slave factories scattered along the West African coast or aboard the ships during the passage, which lasted for several months."⁴ The phrase "were taught" reveals a perhaps willful neglect of the circumstances under which pidgins are acquired and transmitted. Schneider goes on to argue that "we have no reliable information on this." In effect, he refuses to accept the myriad attestations to the pidgin and creole varieties. Although not specifically referring to the literary texts, Salikoko Mufwene writes disparagingly of the theory positing the existence of a "mythical Gullah-like variety."⁵

Having cited many examples, I see no reason to rehash the documentary evidence.⁶ However, even if the historical records are rejected on some principle, there is comparative evidence. Schneider, who seems almost the delegate of the reconstructive tradition dedicated to disproving the creolist theory, has utilized the Works Project Administration (WPA) ex-slave narratives as a beginning, labeling those narratives that were collected in the 1930s "early" black English, despite the fact that attestations are to be found in the early eighteenth century and before. Even allowing for the rejection of those attestations, however, there is enough comparative evidence to support the theory.

Neither has it proved effective to point out the defects in the WPA ex-slave narratives, which in that viewpoint are part of the literary tradition—being collected by untrained workers who were given instructions as to the type of thing they would find and having a disclaimer as to their linguistic utility even from Rawick, the editor of the great mass of the published narratives.⁷ It is necessary, established opinion holds, to cite only evidence from what has been recorded and is available to be heard and analyzed by a contemporary linguist. I do not believe that such a constraint has been placed on any other variety in the entire field of historical linguistics. Recordings of the ex-slave narratives exist—as do other recordings of black speech made in the 1930s, although usually not by septuagenarians—but there is great disagreement as to their transcription by linguists.⁸

Schneider uses the ex-slave narratives, which were collected in the 1930s but claimed to represent the dialect of the preemancipation period because the informants were alive in 1865, to indicate that there are only slight differences from other dialects of American English. The strongest evidence, that of "been verb," (as in "you been know that," meaning "You have known that for a comparatively long time.") is dismissed on the grounds that "regularly" it is used only by one informant, a person from the southeastern South Carolina area who is therefore apparently considered as a speaker of or influenced by Gullah and who is known to have used preverbal "been" in a nonpassive structure. Schneider examines past tense, past participle, perfective auxiliary complex, progressive aspect, etc., but strangely does not consider the most discussed feature of Black English Vernacular (BEV), "be" V-ing, as in "he be joking."[9]

Schneider deals only at the morphological or phrasal level, ignoring matters that have been dealt with best by Marvin Loflin (all references), involving negation, imbedding, conjoining, and other factors of syntax. Nevertheless, Schneider recognizes that "we do find structures that are unquestionably creole or creole-influenced in character" in the past (see the many examples in the works cited in footnote 1) in the plantation South and, apparently, apart from Gullah.[10] He regards the creolized variety, however, as having been limited in scope.

The dialect geographer group that Schneider's work most closely resembles has never dealt adequately with Gullah. Raven McDavid and Virginia McDavid consider it perhaps always to have been limited to the low country or Sea Island area of Georgia and South Carolina. Raven McDavid sees the influence of Gullah in the city of Charleston as limited to a few nonstandard verb forms.[11]

McDavid's article and the extensive body of work that seems to treat it as a starting point ignore the work of Ian F. Hancock on Texan Gullah, specifically that spoken in Bracketville, Texas, at old Fort Clark by the Bracketville "Seminoles." Moved west in the Seminole removal of 1837, the African American speakers of Seminole Gullah, whose speech had almost no Native American characteristics except the use of translated Seminole names such as Warrior, Wildcat, and Bowlegs, carried that variety into Mexico, El Nacimiento, among other places. Even the Bracketville group is said to be proficient in Spanish as well as in a more nearly standard variety of English.[12]

These Afro-Seminoles, according to Hancock, speak a variety of Gullah which seems to have been used in Florida at the time of removal. It is not, however, now identical with the more familiar Gullah of the Charleston area, but this might be expected from almost a century and a half of separation and from the intimate contact of Seminole Gullah with Mexican Spanish and perhaps even Native American languages. It does not have the preverbal particle "blan," a Gullah form for an iterated action, which must have come into "mainstream" Gullah after removal; Hancock traces it to the later influence of Krio, the English creole now localized in Sierra Leone. Postnounal (plural marker "dem"), specialized to a (+human) environment (i.e., "the men" may be rendered as "man dem") may occur after any noun phrase in Sea Island Gullah. Hancock freely uses the term "decreolization." In some respects Seminole creole is more decreolized than Sea Island Gullah is, and in some respects less. He argues that "there is a high consistency of occurrence of prephrasal *duh*, now rare in Gullah."[13] Almost undoubtedly, these changes took place between 1840 and Hancock's fieldwork in the 1970s.

There have, then, been creolized varieties of English (not to mention Louisiana French creole) in two widely separated areas of the United States. Hancock's contention that Krio, the creolized English of Sierra Leone, had a later influence on Gullah would be support for the notion that contact varieties from outside the United States played a role in the history of American English. Spoken by African Americans almost exclusively, these two geographic varieties can certainly be dated earlier than the birth of the oldest contributor to the ex-slave narratives, although Schneider refers to what those ex-slave informants give evidence for as "early" black English.[14]

Of course, the claim that Africans came to the Charleston/Sea Island area bringing pidginized and/or creolized versions of English has not been the point of, nor motivated, all the controversy. The assertion that widespread areas of the American South had such varieties spoken by field-hand slaves is, however, a point of contention.

Let us return, as a preliminary step, to neutral ground—to the Seminole creole studies of Hancock, who has never really committed himself in print on the black English/African American vernacular English/Ebonics issue. Hancock, who has seen equivalent rules in many Afro-creole varieties although with emphasis on English-derived varieties, writes of Seminole creole, "Unmarked verbs usually have past reference." He gives as examples, among others, "mi no du It" (I didn't do it) and "a:tuh dem go hum" (afterwards, they went home).[15]

John Holm indicates the existence of Central American forms "without reference to tense."[16] Lawrence Foster, a far less proficient researcher than Hancock—at least in the linguistic sense—records: "Later Wild Cat took sick with de pox and he die.... she didn't stand back and dey go yonder...."[17] Another way of stating the same category would be that a verbal auxiliary is generic, that is, unmarked with respect to tense.[18] "Generic" refers to an "uninflected" form (sit + O instead of "sat"), which would be considered from the conjoinings with which Loflin worked to have a past reference. Hancock, a less formal linguist than Loflin for all his talent, refers to this form as "O-preterite": "I sit dere and looked at him go" (I sat there . . .).[19]

Marvin Loflin worked with sixteen black or African American informants, six from Washington, D.C., and ten from Saint Louis. His test of generic through conjoinings is a response to criticism of his earlier work on black English, or what he called Negro non-Standard English. His work with co-occurrent adverbs showed rules of the same order—not that past tense could not be marked in the language variety, but that it was not necessarily marked in the proper context.[20]

It was this aspect of Loflin's work that aroused furious opposition. Working in the more conservative tradition of phonological deletion rules, Ralph Fasold found (by my count) eleven phonological rules.[21] It perhaps comes down to a question of taste, but I consider it more parsimonious to write one syntactic rule than eleven strange phonological rules—unless the original intention was to prove that there are no syntactic differences between black English and mainstream American English. I owe to a personal communication from Philip Luelsdorff the observation that such rules imply that the speaker somehow knows Standard English, to which he must apply the deletion rules.

More recent researchers, wishing to keep their terminology as close to that of Standard English as possible but unable to ignore the evidence for this grammatical feature even in the ex-slave narratives, have adopted the term "historical present"—basically a literary term, one would think. It is called "extremely common" in the fairly limited number of recordings that can serve as a corrective to the inexpertly written WPA ex-slave narratives. In Loflin's morphosyntax this verbal category is negated by "ain't." The ex-slave recordings contain "I ain't seed none" and "I ain't read for it 'cause I couldn't read." Myhill also asserts that the "modern AAVE [Afro American Vernacular English]" form would be "I ain't see."[22]

It is not that past-time marking is in any sense missing from the grammar of Gullah, Seminole creole, or black English. Foster records at least eight instances of past-time marking in two short quotations. He also records: "de Injuns most of dem been gone back to de territory" and "we done lost him."[23] The first can possibly be interpreted as "the Indians had been gone . . .," especially since Foster probably did not have Hancock's ability to speak creole English varieties fluently and might not have elicited the "deepest" kind of Seminole creole. But Hancock reports that "the past (anterior) marker is *been*" and gives numerous examples, and he concludes that "the completive aspect marker is *done*."[24] The use of "been" and "done" as such markers, with some variations in function in different varieties, is one of the best-known features of the English pidgin/creole field; there are parallels in French- and Portuguese-based creoles. The creolelike nature of "been" past (anterior) marker in a nonpassive function is one of the few undisputed facts in this controversial field. Schneider finds it "regularly" used by only one informant in the ex-slave narratives—who was from South Carolina and presumably a speaker of or influenced by Gullah—but it is incontestably there "irregularly" in other ex-slaves' interviews.[25] Loflin found it in Washington, D.C., but under such limited conditions that he called it an emphasis marker, and Fasold notes some restrictions.[26] Joan Fickett (in a personal communication with the author) reports multiple usage on the order of "been, been, been" in marking anterior time relationships, which is certainly non-mainstream, although not attested in more basic pidgins and creoles. Changes in a form so strikingly different from the English of surrounding dialects are certainly to be expected.

Acceptance of "been" as a nonpassive anterior marker is tantamount to admission of at least the possibility of earlier creolization, despite arguments as to the widespread nature of the form. Claims have frequently been made that it is limited to South Carolina, as Thomas Wentworth Higginson reported during the Civil War. Higginson's regiment was South Carolinian, and his soldiers may have been speakers of Gullah. (Some of his soldiers, however, came from Florida. He says little about any dialect difference but does say that the Florida soldiers, one of whom is quoted in nearly Standard English, have more house servants among them. Thus, the distinction at the time seems to have been more nearly social—field hands as against house servants—than geographic.) Higginson's more complete knowledge of South Carolina dialect may be the reason for his statement that "'Done' is a Virginia shibboleth, quite distinct from the 'been' which replaces it in South Carolina."[27]

Others, however, place no such geographical limitations.[28] Fickett reports it from Buffalo, New York, with no evidence of in-migration specifically from South Carolina, and Labov reports it from Philadelphia.[29] A student of mine at Northwestern State University in Natchitoches, Louisiana, in the 1980s—a black athlete in a "developmental" English class—wrote (in the context of writing about how he prepared for his final examination): "what I been know about English." There seems to be some tendency in black American English vernacular to restrict this "been" to stative verbs, for example, "I been had it a long time" and "You been know dat." There is also a tendency to restrict especially stressed "been" to emphatic usage, but neither tendency is anywhere complete.

Black English freely combines this "been" with the "-ing" form of the verb, producing sequences such as "They been goin'," which is in mainstream practice dutifully traceable to contraction and deletion rules, from "They have been going" to "They've been going," and then to "They been going." If we look at Sea Island and Seminole Gullah, however, we find "beenuh do."[30] And Hancock gives as an example, "dis yeiz beenuh huht mi ba:d" (This ear has been hurting me badly). He says nothing about "been huhtin" in Seminole Gullah, but he does report, "the English of some of the very old people in particular is clearly influenced by ASC [Afro Seminole Creole]."[31]

Turner records "di bukruh been standin" (the white man had been standing) alongside "beenuh do."[32] Parallel to "duh V-ing" would be "beenuh V-ing," where the "-uh" (reduction of "duh") would cross with the "a-" (from "on," with gerund) as "I'm adoin' it" and would facilitate the adoption of that nonstandard form in the African American community. Higginson records: "my old mudder, Been a-waggin' at de hill so long" or "I been a-thinking," where the placement of the hyphen in the South Carolinian soldier's phrase may reflect Higginson's greater familiarity with white dialect patterns. But Higginson also has "Den I been-a-tink" and "I been-a-tremble" with two hyphens as if to indicate that he is not sure where the division goes.[33]

Hancock reports that Seminole Gullah has the form "-uh" after anterior marker "been."[34] Some of Turner's examples represent "deeper" Gullah than others, and it seems likely that a certain amount of decreolization has taken place. Black English grammar could easily produce "He been standin," and it really seems unnecessary, in the context of comparison to Sea Island and Seminole Gullah, then to insert "have" and then to delete it, whether with intermediate contraction or not, just because ordinary English has that derivation of a comparable sequence.

A comparable, perhaps partly decreolized, example from Hancock will possibly provide some more light: "wa' i duh duin yuh?" (What is he doing there?), although "duh" is usually followed by the simple verb base.[35] Both Sea Island Gullah and Seminole Gullah use "duh gwain."[36] The "-ing" forms would seem to have been modeled after Standard English, to which both Sea Island and Seminole speakers had long been exposed at the time of the fieldwork by both linguists. Hopkins regards this "going" (as well as "coming") in Sea Island Gullah as "having been acquired in their inflected forms" and finds a slightly different relationship, in decreolization, with Standard English "be": "aen ai taat hi wa duh fan" (and I thought he was joking). Hopkins suggests a kind of relationship between "duh V" and "be V-ing," which, developing differently in Sea Island Gullah, Seminole Gullah, Central American English, and black American English, may still involve a syntactic relationship.[37] Holm notes "the proximity [in the company of an outsider] of the two alternate constructions for the progressive: "no de briyd . . . no briydin."[38] Hopkins finds, in fact, "two examples [of] the construction *be* + *-ing*" along with this "transitional phase."[39] John Rickford has linked this form effectively to the decreolization process.[40] The situation is reminiscent of, although not identical to, that of urban Papiamentu, where "ta skucha" (is listening) can become "ta skuchando" under the influence of Spanish, which is used daily in Willemstad.[41]

Support for a general consensus that black English is syntactically different from ordinary English can be seen in forms such as "I be catchin'," which contrasts, in terms of co-occurrent time expressions and other factors, with "I catchin'" even if it be allowed, for the purpose of argument, that "am" has been contracted and then deleted. Although attempts to relate black English to mainstream dialects have tried to emphasize the present-tense function of this form, it clearly has a past-tense potential. There are occurrences such as "He be dancin' last Friday," and Loflin presents extensive additional evidence.[42] Working with conjoinings, something hardly attempted by conventional dialectologists, he comes up with sentences such as "You be talkin' to somebody and they was talkin' all loud" and "they be quiet and I won." Here it is especially important to note the highly marked quality of black English "be."[43] In an unmarked context, it is quite possible for the same speakers to say "You was talkin' to somebody and they was talkin' all loud" and "They was quiet and I won."

The early—really early, not ex-slave—attestations of black English in Hugh Henry Brackenridge's *Modern Chivalry* include a quote from Cuff (from Cuffee, possibly the day name for Friday): "I be cash crabs in the river Wye." Here Cuff is clearly reporting a past event but one continuing over a period of time—fishing (or crabbing) is not something done in an instant.[44] The thesis here is that, in adapting to the Standard English of his auditors (the philosophical society), Cuff avoids "duh" but has not learned Standard English syntax and therefore can supply only a word-for-word substitution, "be" for "duh." At this point "I be catch" is a more likely decreolized form than "I be catching," but it is a simple matter to add the participial ending. "Duh" in Gullah "is used in a present, past, even future sense, dependent upon the context."[45] Loflin does not deal with it directly, but he does cite forms such as "She be dere in fifteen or twenty minutes."[46] Many have noted similar usages in nonelicitation situations with black English speakers. For instance, Patricia Jones-Jackson quotes a Gullah speaker, acropetally in a future context, "I be please[d]."[47] Examples are everywhere.

Loflin, incidentally, in earlier stages of his analysis had three derivations for "be." In the first, "will be" underwent contraction to "'l be" and then deletion to "be." In the second, "would be" became "'d be" and then "be" by contraction and deletion. In the third, "be" was the underlying (basic) form without the stages of contraction and deletion. He later abandoned this scheme. Although Fasold wonders at this "defection," it was obviously

Loflin's work on conjoinings and sequence of tense that led him to his later, more creolelike formulation.[48]

Sea Island Gullah, Bracketville Gullah, Central American English, and American black English are obviously not identical, nor may they have been identical at any time in the past. Different environments, however, may account for some of the differences. The history of the preverbal particles, the grammatical functions of those particles—different from any white dialect forms—and the unmarked tense (depending upon other factors for an indication of whether the action referred to is present or past) indicate, however, striking similarities. There are many other factors, but space does not permit discussion here.

Since Seminole Gullah could not have been separated from Sea Island Gullah before the latter developed, an origin at least as early as 1800—and probably earlier—is indicated. *Pace* Mufwene, American black English is historically "Gullah-like" in some of the ways discussed above. The attestations point to its development earlier than 1800, probably still in the colonial period. Not every report of peculiarities of black speech can be taken as certain evidence of a creolelike variety, but the opposite—that it necessarily points to a British regional usage—could hardly be said to be true.

There were apparently noncreolized, less "deviant" uses of English among the slave populations, particularly among the house servants. Slaves' speech in the more northerly states, although regarded as having some characteristics of social dialect, may not have been of a creolized or even a near-creolized variety.[49] The freed slaves who went to Samaná, Dominican Republic, around 1824 provide a challenge to a simple, blanket decreolization model.[50] At least equal weight, however, should be given to the creole English carried to the Bahamas by "American loyalists and their slaves"; the latter had by 1788 "more than doubled the Bahamas' total population and trebled that of the blacks."[51] And some weight should be given to the settler English of Liberia, the speech of descendants of nineteenth-century "repatriates" to Liberia, which Hancock calls a "vestigial creole."[52] Holm's work is—perhaps conveniently—omitted from the list of "studies of people of African heritage outside of the United States."[53]

Much more work has to be done before we can pinpoint these strikingly similar varieties within a matter of decades. It seems clear, however, that they had developed by the late colonial or early postcolonial period, if not much earlier. However much recent divergence—or redivergence—there may be in places such as inner-city Philadelphia, creolization in American black English can hardly be hidden under the facade of (re)divergence in the post–World War II period.

Pedagogical implications may depend upon the historical issue more than is usually thought. Fasold, devoted to the Anglocentric approach and to minimizing syntactic differences, considered briefly the possibility that the sentence "He might be home now," which would be generated by both the ordinary American English and black English vernacular grammars, might mean different things to speakers of the two dialects. He concluded that such an eventuality was "extremely doubtful" and set about to find "a syntactic explanation for the Black English usage."[54] If, however, the sequence—and others like it—has two different histories (syntactic and chronological), then the possibilities for unsuspected misunderstandings may be great.

Notes

1. Donald Winford, "Common Ground and Creole TMA," *Journal of Pidgin and Creole Languages* 11, no. 1 (1996): 71–87; William Labov, *The Social Stratification of English in New York City* (Washington, D.C.: Center for Applied Linguistics, 1965); William Labov, Paul Cohen, Clarence Robins, and John Lewis, *A Study of the Nonstandard English of Negro and Puerto Rican Speakers in New York City* (Washington, D.C.: U.S. Office of Education, Cooperative Research Project No. 3288, 1968); Beryl L. Bailey, "Towards New Perspective in Negro English Dialectology," *American Speech* 40, no. 1 (1965): 32–40; William A. Stewart, "Sociolinguistic Factors in the History of American Negro Dialects," *Florida Foreign Language Reporter* 5, no. 2 (1967): 11–29; "Continuity and Change in American Negro Dialects," *Florida Foreign Language Reporter* 6, no. 2 (1968): 3–14; Guy Bailey, "Are Black and White Vernaculars Diverging?," *American Speech* 62, no. 1 (1987): 32–40.

2. George Philip Krapp, *The English Language in America*, vol. 1 (New York: Frederick Ungar, 1925), pp. 225–73; James Blanding Haman, "The Growth of the Use of Negro Dialect in American Verse and Short Story" (master's thesis, Duke University, 1939).

3. Anthropologist Emanuel Drechsel, in a personal communication with the author, pointed out that all of the recorders were speakers of English, but not by any means were all native speakers. See Michel Guillaume Jean de Crevecoeur, *Letters from an American Farmer* (London, 1782); Gustav Dresel, *Houston Journal: Adventures in North America and Texas, 1837–1841* [trans. from German by Max Freund] (Austin: Texas University Press, 1954).

4. Edgar W. Schneider, *Earlier American Black English* (Tuscaloosa: University of Alabama Press, 1989), p. 31. A corrective to this attitude could be found in J. Graham Cruickshank, *Black Talk* (Demarara, Guyana: Argosy Co., 1916):

"*Matty a larn matty*" (a slave taught a fellow slave [little by little]). This passage emphasizes the peer transmission that is so important at all stages of pidginization and creolization.

5. Salikoko S. Mufwene, "The Development of American Englishes: Some Questions from a Creole Genesis Perspective," in *Focus on the USA*, ed. Edgar W. Schneider (Amsterdam: John Benjamins, 1995), p. 243.

6. J. L. Dillard, "On the Beginnings of Black English in the United States," *Orbis* 21, no. 2 (1972): 523–36; J. L. Dillard, *Black English, Its History and Usage in the United States* (New York: Random House, 1972); J. L. Dillard, *All-American English* (New York: Random House, 1974); J. L. Dillard, *Toward a Social History of American English* (Berlin: deGruyter, 1981); J. L. Dillard, *A History of American English* (Essex: Longman, 1992). See also Beryl Bailey, *Towards New Perspective;* Stewart, *Sociolinguistic Factors;* and Doublas B. Chambers, "'He Is an African but Speaks Plain': Historical Creolization in Eighteenth-Century Virginia," in *The African Diaspora*, ed. Alusine Jalloh and Stephen E. Maizlish (College Station: Texas A&M University Press, 1996), pp. 100–33.

7. J. L. Dillard, "The Relative Value of the Ex-Slave Narratives," in *Africanisms in Afro-American Language Varieties*, ed. Salikoko S. Mufwene (Athens: University of Georgia Press, 1993), pp. 222–31. John Lomax's directive is printed in Jerre G. Mangione, *The Dream and the Deal: The Federal Writers' Project* (Philadelphia: University of Pennsylvania Press, 1983). It is interesting that Lomax's instructions to the WPA interviewers are the only independent evidence of a concerted attempt—a "conspiracy"—to represent African American speech in a specified way. Thus, the ex-slave narratives would seem not to be a corrective to any kind of literary conspiracy but the only example of such a conspiracy.

8. John Myhill, "The Use of Features of Present-Day AAVE in the Ex-Slave Recordings," *American Speech* (1995): 141.

9. Schneider, *Earlier American Black English*, p. 278. For rare use of "been V" in written texts, see Joan M. Fayer, "Nigerian Pidgin English in Old Calabar in the Eighteenth and Nineteenth Centuries," in *Pidgin and Creole Tense-Mood=Aspect Systems*, ed. John Victor Singler (Amsterdam: John Benjamins, 1990), pp. 196–98.

10. Schneider, *Earlier American Black English*, p. 278.

11. Raven I. McDavid, Jr., and Virginia Glenn McDavid, "The Relationship of the Speech of American Negroes to the Speech of Whites," *American Speech* 26 (1951): 3–17; Raven I. McDavid, Jr., "The Position of the Charleston Dialect," *Publications of the American Dialect Society* 23 (1953): 35–49. Note that this publication is not in Schneider's bibliography.

12. Ian F. Hancock, "The Creole English of the Bracketville Afro-Seminoles," in *Perspectives on American English*, ed. J. L. Dillard (The Hague: Mouton, 1980), p. 309.

13. Ibid., p. 324. Hancock's transcriptions, like other transcriptions of Gullah in which the linguist employs special symbols, have been adapted to a more conventional orthography herein, on the basis that phonology is not here the critical issue. Hancock provides a precedent in his "Afro-Seminole Word List," *Seminole Quarterly* 1, no. 1 (1992).

14. Ian F. Hancock, "Gullah and Barbadian, Origins and Relationships," *American Speech* 54, no. 3 (1979): 33–48; J. L. Dillard, *A History of American English* (Es-

sex: Longman, 1992), see especially chap. 5; Schneider, *Earlier American Black English*, pp. 42–61.

15. Hancock, "Creole English," p. 323.
16. John Holm, *Central American English* (Heidelberg: Julius Gross Verlag, 1983), p. 105. This feature is widely reported in Afro-pidgins and creoles; see Fayer, "Nigerian Pidgin English," p. 190, and John Victor Singler, "The Impact of Decreolization upon T-M-A; Tenseless, Mood, and Aspect in Kru Pidgin English," in Singler, "Impact of Decreolization," p. 208.
17. Lawrence Foster, "Negro-Indian Relationships in the Southwest" (Ph.D. diss., University of Pennsylvania, 1935), pp. 43, 48.
18. Marvin D. Loflin, "Black American English and Syntactic Dialectology," in *Perspectives on Black English*, ed. J. L. Dillard (The Hague: Mouton, 1974), pp. 65–73.
19. Hancock, "Creole English," p. 314. E. Bagby Atwood was probably the first researcher to notice this feature, but he did not dwell on it or suggest rules or even a designation for it; see E. Bagby Atwood, *A Survey of Verb Forms in the Eastern United States* (Ann Arbor: University of Michigan Press, 1953).
20. Marvin D. Loflin, "On the Structure of the Verb in a Dialect of American Negro English," *Linguistics* 59 (1970): 14–28. This is almost the earliest principle of creole grammar, being evident—although not made explicit—in the work of J. J. Thomas, *The Theory and Practice of Creole Grammar* (London: New Beacon Books, 1862/1969). Cf. Singler, "Impact of Decreolization," p. 208: "Thus, when the sentence in (8) is divorced from context, it is not possible to know whether the action it refers to is past or nonpast."
21. Ralph W. Fasold, *Tense Marking in Black English* (Washington, D.C.: Center for Applied Linguistics, 1972), pp. 38–120.
22. Myhill, "Use of Features," pp. 119, 124, passim.
23. Foster, "Negro-Indian Relationships," p. 43.
24. Hancock, "Creole English," p. 325.
25. Schneider, *Earlier American Black English*, p. 275.
26. Marvin D. Loflin, "On the Passive in Nonstandard English," *Journal of English as a Second Language* 4 (1969): 19–23; Ralph W. Fasold, *The Sociolinguistics of Language* (Oxford and Cambridge: Blackwells, 1990), pp. 208–209.
27. Thomas Wentworth Higginson, *Army Life in a Black Regiment* (New York: Collier Books, 1869/1962).
28. For a really broad viewpoint, see Jan Voorhoeve, "Historical and Linguistic Evidence in Favour of the Relexification Theory in the Formation of Creoles," *Language in Society* 2 (1973): 133–45. Some of Voorhoeve's data have been subjected to criticism, e.g., his indication of "taba" as a parallel to "been" in Papiamentu. Modern Papiamentu is apparently restricted to "tabata," parallel to "beenuh"; but folktales often begin with the formula "tabatin" ("taba [past marker] plus "tin" [have]).
29. Joan G. Fickett, "Aspects of Morphemics, Syntax, and Semology of an Inner-City Dialect" (Ph.D. diss., State University of New York at Buffalo, 1970); William Labov, *Language in the Inner City* (Philadelphia: University of Pennsylvania Press, 1972), pp. 53–55.
30. Lorenzo Dow Turner, *Africanisms in the Gullah Dialect* (Chicago: University of Chicago Pres, 1949), p. 225. As with other Gullah and Seminole Gullah mate-

rials, phonological transcriptions have been adapted to more conventional orthography.

31. Hancock, "Creole English," pp. 324, 321.
32. Turner, *Africanisms*, pp. 272, 225.
33. Higginson, *Army Life*, p. 197, p. 33, p. 37, respectively.
34. Hancock, "Creole English," p. 324.
35. Ibid., p. 327.
36. Turner, *Africanisms*, p. 213; Hancock, "Creole English," p. 324.
37. Tometro Hopkins, "The Auxiliary Verb *da* in Contemporary Gullah," in *The Crucible of Carolina, Essays in the Development of Gullah Language and Culture*, ed. Michael Montgomery (Athens: University of Georgia Press, 1994), p. 73.
38. Holm, *Central American English*, p. 11. A similar situation apparently obtains also in Trinidad. Barbara Lalla's review of Lise Winer, *Trinidad and Tobago* (Amsterdam: John Benjamins, 1993) in *Journal of Pidgin and Creole Languages* 11, no. 2 (1996): p. 369, reports a "period of redundancy in which both "da" and "-in" occurred together."
39. Hopkins, *Auxiliary Verb*, p. 73.
40. John Rickford, "The Insights of the Mesolect," in *Pidgins and Creoles: Current Trends and Prospects*, ed. Ian F. Hancock and David DeCamp (Washington, D.C.: Georgetown University Press, 1974), p. 109. One of the strange features of a strange field is the frequently expressed notion that Rickford found Irish influence in this "be." Although he considered that possibility, he clearly concluded that if there was any Irish influence, "it was indirect."
41. Richard Wood, "The Hispanization of a Creole Language," *Hispania* 55 (1972): 857–64.
42. Marvin D. Loflin, Nicholas Sobin, and J. L. Dillard, "Auxiliary Structures and Time Adverbs in Black American English," *American Speech* 48 (1973): 22–36.
43. Marvin D. Loflin, *Black American English: Independent Motivation for the Auxiliary Hypothesis*, Technical Report No. 2, Institute for the Study of Urban Linguistics (Madison: University of Wisconsin, 1972).
44. Hugh Henry Brackenridge, *Modern Chivalry* (New Haven, Conn.: College & University Press, 1792/1965), p. 130.
45. Turner, *Africanisms*, p. 213. From the ex-slave recordings, consider: "If you be do the wrong thing, and they sen' me after you, only reason I won' get you, I won't see you" (quoted in Myhill, "Use of Features," p. 123). Consider also: "I be damn" (quoted in Ibid., p. 141).
46. Loflin, *Black American English*, pp. 65–73. It is noteworthy that Cuff (in Brackenridge, *Modern Chivalry*, p. 130) uses a future-reference "be": "[I] be a filasafa [in the city, to which he is going]."
47. Patricia Jones-Jackson, *When Roots Die* (Athens: University of Georgia Press, 1987), p. 86; see also p. 141.
48. Fasold, *Tense Marking*, p. 184.
49. Justice Daniel P. Horsmanden reported, in his 1744 account, a "dialect so perfectly negro" that an interpreter was required; but two sons-in-law of his master had learned to understand him and could interpret for him. See Daniel P. Horsmanden, *The New York Conspiracy* (Boston: Beacon Press, 1971), p. 146.

50. Shana Poplack and David Sankoff, "The Philadelphia Story in the Caribbean," *American Speech* 62, no. 4 (1987): 291–314; Sali Tagliamonte and Shana Poplack, "How Black English Past Got To Be Present: Evidence from Samana," *Language in Society* 17, no. 4(1988): 513–34.

51. John Holm, "African Elements in White Bahamian English," *English World-Wide* 1, no. 1 (1980): 48. See also Holm's table of creole characteristics on p. 60. Of the latter only "de" (here labeled "progressive") and "did done" ("Anterior Completive") are unmatched in BEV. The former, however, varies in Holm's table, with "-in," which certainly occurs in BEV. Only the replacement of "de" with "be," extensively discussed above, is not indicated in Holm's data.

52. Ian F. Hancock, "Some Aspects of English in Liberia," *Liberian Studies Journal* 3 (1971): 207–13.

53. Myhill, "Use of Features," p. 116.

54. Fasold, *Tense Marking*, p. 177.